The Supporters' Guide to Non-League Football 2007

EDITOR
John Robinson

Fifteenth Edition

For details of our range of over 1,300 books and 250 DVDs, visit our web site or contact us using the information shown below.

British Library Cataloguing in Publication Data
A catalogue record for this book is available from the British Library

ISBN-10: 1-86223-148-6
ISBN-13: 978-1-86223-148-1   (for use after January 2007)

Manufactured in the UK by LPPS Ltd, Wellingborough, NN8 3PJ

FOREWORD

Our thanks go to the numerous club officials who have aided us in the compilation of information contained in this guide and also to Michael Robinson (page layouts), Bob Budd (cover artwork) and Tony Brown (Cup Statistics – www.soccerdata.com) for the part they have played.

Although we use the term 'Child' for concessionary prices, this is usually the price charged to Senior Citizens also.

Wherever possible we have included web site information as a new item but, to date, not all clubs have this facility.

Following the latest reorganisation of the Non-League Pyramid structure, we have confined this guide to the 68 Football Conference Clubs in Steps 1 & 2. Our other Non-League guide covering Step 3 level clubs will be published in September 2006 and we would like to wish our readers a happy and safe spectating season.

At the time of going to press several clubs were in a precarious financial position including Crawley Town FC which was in administration. On the basis that the Conference fixtures include such clubs we have provided full details on the assumption that the clubs will be able to fulfil their obligations.

John Robinson
EDITOR

CONTENTS

The Nationwide Football Conference National Clubs

Address Riverside House, 14B High Street,
Crayford, Kent   DA1 4HG

Phone (01322) 411021   **Fax** (01322) 411022

Clubs for the 2006/2007 Season

ALDERSHOT TOWN FC

Founded: 1992
Former Names: Aldershot FC
Nickname: 'Shots'
Ground: Recreation Ground, High Street, Aldershot, GU11 1TW
Record Attendance: 7,500 (18/11/2000)
Pitch Size: 117 × 76 yards

Colours: Shirts are Red and Blue Quarters, Red shorts
Telephone Nº: (01252) 320211
Fax Number: (01252) 324347
Club Secretary: (01252) 337065 – Andrew Morgan
Ground Capacity: 7,500
Seating Capacity: 1,885
Web site: www.theshots.co.uk

GENERAL INFORMATION

Supporters Club: c/o Club
Telephone Nº: (01252) 320211
Car Parking: Municipal Car Park is adjacent
Coach Parking: Contact the club for information
Nearest Railway Station: Aldershot (5 mins. walk)
Nearest Bus Station: Aldershot (5 minutes walk)
Club Shop: At the ground
Opening Times: Matchdays only
Telephone Nº: (01252) 320211
Police Telephone Nº: (01252) 324545

GROUND INFORMATION

Away Supporters' Entrances & Sections:
Accommodation in the East Bank Terrace

ADMISSION INFO (2006/2007 PRICES)

Adult Standing: £12.00
Adult Seating: £15.00
Child Standing: £7.00
Child Seating: £8.00
Senior Citizen Standing: £7.00
Senior Citizen Seating: £8.00
Programme Price: £2.50

DISABLED INFORMATION

Wheelchairs: Accommodated in a covered area
Helpers: Admitted
Prices: Free for the disabled. Helpers charged £5.00
Disabled Toilets: None
Contact: (01252) 320211 (Bookings are necessary)

Travelling Supporters' Information:
Routes: From the M3: Exit at Junction 4 and follow signs for Aldershot (A331). Leave the A331 at the A323 exit (Ash Road) and continue along into the High Street. The ground is just past the Railway Bridge on the right; From the A31: Continue along the A31 to the junction with the A331, then as above; From the A325 (Farnborough Road): Follow signs to the A323 then turn left into Wellington Avenue. The ground is just off the 2nd roundabout on the left – the floodlights are clearly visible.

ALTRINCHAM FC

Founded: 1903
Former Names: None
Nickname: 'The Robins'
Ground: Moss Lane, Altrincham   WA15 8AP
Record Attendance: 10,275 (February 1925)
Pitch Size: 110 × 74 yards

Colours: Red and White striped shirts, Black shorts
Telephone Nº: (0161) 928-1045
Daytime Phone Nº: (0161) 928-1045
Fax Number: (0161) 926-9934
Ground Capacity: 6,085
Seating Capacity: 1,154
Web site: www.altrinchamfc.com

GENERAL INFORMATION

Supporters Trust: Brian Flynn, STAR, c/o Club
Telephone Nº: –
Car Parking: Adjacent to the ground
Coach Parking: By Police Direction
Nearest Railway Station: Altrincham (5 minutes walk)
Nearest Bus Station: Altrincham
Club Shop: At the ground
Opening Times: 9.00am – 5.00pm Matchdays & Weekdays
Telephone Nº: (0161) 928-1045
Police Telephone Nº: (0161) 872-5050

GROUND INFORMATION

Away Supporters' Entrances & Sections:
Richmans End turnstiles and accommodation

ADMISSION INFO (2006/2007 PRICES)

Adult Standing: £10.00
Adult Seating: £12.00
Child Standing: £6.00
Child Seating: £7.00
Under-11s: £2.00
Programme Price: £2.00

DISABLED INFORMATION

Wheelchairs: 3 spaces are available each for home and away fans adjacent to the Away dugout
Helpers: Admitted
Prices: Free for the disabled. £10.00 for helpers
Disabled Toilets: Yes
Contact: (0161) 928-1045   (Bookings are necessary)

Travelling Supporters' Information:
Routes: Exit the M56 at Junction 7, following signs for Hale and Altrincham. Go through the 1st main set of traffic lights and take the 3rd right into Westminster Road and continue into Moss Lane. The ground is on the right.

BURTON ALBION FC

Founded: 1950
Former Names: None
Nickname: 'The Brewers'
Ground: The Pirelli Stadium, Princess Way, Burton-on-Trent   DE13 0AR
Record Attendance: 6,000 (8th January 2006)
Pitch Size: 110 × 72 yards

Colours: Shirts are Yellow with Black trim, shorts are Black with Yellow Trim
Telephone Nº: 0870 190-0060
Fax Number: (01283) 523199
Ground Capacity: 6,000
Seating Capacity: 2,000
Web site: www.burtonalbionfc.co.uk

GENERAL INFORMATION

Supporters Club: c/o Club
Telephone Nº: 0870 190-0060
Car Parking: Available at the ground
Coach Parking: Rykneld Trading Estate, Derby Road
Nearest Railway Station: Burton-on-Trent (1½ miles)
Nearest Bus Station: Burton-on-Trent (1½ miles)
Club Shop: At the ground
Opening Times: Weekdays 9.00am – 5.00pm and Matchdays from 1½ hours before kick-off
Telephone Nº: 0870 190-0060
Police Telephone Nº: (08543) 302010

GROUND INFORMATION

Away Supporters' Entrances & Sections:
East Stand, Derby Road

ADMISSION INFO (2006/2007 PRICES)

Adult Standing: £12.00
Adult Seating: £14.00
Child Standing: £3.00
Child Seating: £5.00
Senior Citizen Standing: £10.00
Senior Citizen Seating: £12.00
Programme Price: £2.00

DISABLED INFORMATION

Wheelchairs: Over 78 spaces available for home and away fans in the designated disabled areas
Helpers: Admitted
Prices: Normal prices for the disabled. Free for helpers
Disabled Toilets: Available in all stands
Contact: 0870 190-0060   (Bookings are necessary)

Travelling Supporters' Information:
Routes: From the M1, North and South: Exit at Junction 23A and join the A50 towards Derby (also signposted for Alton Towers). Join the A38 southbound at the Toyota factory (towards Burton & Lichfield) then exit for Burton North onto the A5121. Continue past the Pirelli factory on the right and the BP Garage and Cash & Carry on the left then turn into Princess Way at the roundabout; From the M5/6 South: Join the M42 northbound and exit onto the A446 signposted Lichfield. Follow signs for the A38 to Burton then exit onto A5121 as above; From the M6 North: Exit at Junction 15 and follow the A50 towards Stoke and Uttoxeter. Exit the A50 for the A38 southbound signposted Burton and Lichfield at the Toyota factory, then as above.

CAMBRIDGE UNITED FC

Founded: 1912
Former Name: Abbey United FC (1912-1951)
Nickname: 'U's' 'United'
Ground: Abbey Stadium, Newmarket Road, Cambridge   CB5 8LN
Ground Capacity: 8,696
Seating Capacity: 4,376

Pitch Size: 110 × 72 yards
Record Attendance: 14,000 (1/5/70)
Colours: Amber shirts, Black shorts
Telephone Nº: (01223) 566500
Ticket Office: (01223) 566500
Fax Number: (01223) 566502
Web Site: www.cambridgeunited.com

GENERAL INFORMATION

Car Parking: –
Coach Parking: Coldhams Road
Nearest Railway Station: Cambridge (2 miles)
Nearest Bus Station: Cambridge City Centre
Club Shop: At the ground
Opening Times: Monday to Friday 9.00am to 5.00pm and Matchdays 11.00am to kick-off
Telephone Nº: (01223) 566500
Police Telephone Nº: (01223) 358966

GROUND INFORMATION

Away Supporters' Entrances & Sections:
Coldham Common turnstiles 20-22 – Habbin Terrace (South) and South Stand (Seating) turnstiles 23-26

ADMISSION INFO (2006/2007 PRICES)

Adult Standing: £12.00
Adult Seating: £15.00
Child Standing: £3.00
Child Seating: £3.00 (in the Family Stand) or £7.00
Concessionary Standing: £8.00
Concessionary Seating: £10.00
Programme Price: £2.50

DISABLED INFORMATION

Wheelchairs: 19 spaces in total for Home fans in the disabled sections, in front of Main Stand and in the North Terrace. 16 spaces for Away fans in the South Stand.
Helpers: One helper admitted per disabled fan
Prices: £8.00 for the disabled. Free of charge for helpers
Disabled Toilets: At the rear of the disabled section
Contact: (01223) 566500 (Bookings are necessary)

Travelling Supporters' Information: Routes: From the North: Take the A1 and A14 to Cambridge and then head towards Newmarket. Turn off onto the B1047, signposted for Cambridge Airport, Horningsea and Fen Ditton. Turn right at the top of the slip road and travel through Fen Ditton. Turn right at the traffic lights at the end of the village. Go straight on at the roundabout onto Newmarket Road. The ground is 500 yards on the left; From the South and East: Take the A10 or A130 to the M11. Head North to the A14. Then as from the North; From the West: Take the A422 to Cambridge and join the A14. Then as from North.
Bus Services: Services from the Railway Station to the City Centre and Nº 3 from the City Centre to the Ground.

CRAWLEY TOWN FC

Note: At the time of our going to press the club had entered administration with the possibility that it would not compete during the 2006/2007 season.

Founded: 1896
Former Names: None
Nickname: 'Red Devils'
Ground: Broadfield Stadium, Brighton Road, Crawley, Sussex   RH11 9RX
Record Attendance: 4,516 (2004)
Pitch Size: 110 × 72 yards

Colours: Red shirts and shorts
Telephone Nº: (01293) 410000 (Ground)
Daytime Nº: (01293) 410000
Fax Number: (01293) 410002
Ground Capacity: 4,941
Seating Capacity: 1,150
Web site: None

GENERAL INFORMATION

Supporters Club: Alain Harper, 33 Nuthurst Close, Ifield, Crawley, Sussex
Telephone Nº: (01293) 511764
Car Parking: 350 spaces available at the ground
Coach Parking: At the ground
Nearest Railway Station: Crawley (1 mile)
Nearest Bus Station: By the Railway Station
Club Shop: At the ground
Opening Times: Weekdays and matchdays 9.00am–5.00pm
Telephone Nº: (01293) 410000
Police Telephone Nº: (08456) 070999

GROUND INFORMATION

Away Supporters' Entrances & Sections: No usual segregation

ADMISSION INFO (2006/2007 PRICES)

Adult Standing: £11.00
Adult Seating: £13.00
Concessionary Standing: £7.00
Concessionary Seating: £9.00
Junior Reds: £4.00 Seating; Standing is free of charge
Programme Price: £2.00

DISABLED INFORMATION

Wheelchairs: Accommodated in the disabled section of the Main Stand (Lift access available)
Helpers: One helper admitted per disabled fan
Prices: Normal prices apply
Disabled Toilets: Available
Contact: (01293) 410000   (Bookings are not necessary)

Travelling Supporters' Information:
Routes: Exit the M23 at Junction 11 and take the A23 towards Crawley. After ¼ mile, the Stadium is on the left. Take the first exit at the roundabout for the Stadium entrance.

DAGENHAM & REDBRIDGE FC

Founded: 1992
Former Names: Formed by the merger of Dagenham FC and Redbridge Forest FC
Nickname: 'The Daggers'
Ground: Glyn Hopkin Stadium, Victoria Road, Dagenham, Essex   RM10 7XL
Record Attendance: 7,100 (1967)
Pitch Size: 110 × 65 yards

Colours: Red shirts with White shorts
Telephone Nº: (0208) 592-1549
Office Phone Nº: (0208) 592-7194
Secretary's Phone Nº: (0208) 592-7194
Fax Number: (0208) 593-7227
Ground Capacity: 6,077
Seating Capacity: 1,015
Web site: www.daggers.co.uk

GENERAL INFORMATION
Supporters Club: Russell Elmes, 24 Brewood, Dagenham, RM8 2BL
Telephone Nº: (0208) 593-2801
Car Parking: Street parking only
Coach Parking: Street parking only
Nearest Railway Station: Dagenham East (5 mins. walk)
Nearest Bus Station: Romford
Club Shop: At the ground
Opening Times: Matchdays only
Telephone Nº: (0208) 592-7194
Police Telephone Nº: (0208) 593-8232

GROUND INFORMATION
Away Supporters' Entrances & Sections:
Pondfield Road entrances for Pondfield Road End

ADMISSION INFO (2006/2007 PRICES)
Adult Standing: £12.00
Adult Seating: £14.00
Under-16s Standing: £6.00
Child Seating: £9.00 (£6.00 in the Family Stand)
Senior Citizen Seating: £7.00 in the Family Stand
Family Tickets: £21.00 – 2 adults + 1 children (Family Stand)
Programme Price: £2.50

DISABLED INFORMATION
Wheelchairs: Accommodated in front of new Stand
Helpers: Admitted
Prices: £5.00 for the disabled. Free of charge for Helpers
Disabled Toilets: Available at the East and West ends of the ground and also in the Clubhouse
Contact: (0208) 592-7194   (Bookings are necessary)

Travelling Supporters' Information:
Routes: From the North & West: Take the M11 to its end and join the A406 South. At the large roundabout take the slip road on the left signposted A13 to Dagenham. As you approach Dagenham, stay in the left lane and follow signs for A1306 signposted Dagenham East. Turn left onto the A1112 at the 3rd set of traffic lights by the McDonalds. Proceed along Ballards Road to The Bull roundabout and bear left. Victoria Road is 450 yards on the left after passing Dagenham East tube station; From the South & East: Follow signs for the A13 to Dagenham. Take the next slip road off signposted Elm Park & Dagenham East then turn right at the roundabout. Go straight on at the next roundabout and turn left onto A1306. After ½ mile you will see a McDonalds on the right. Get into the right hand filter lane and turn right onto A1112. Then as from the North & West.

EXETER CITY FC

Founded: 1904
Former Names: Formed by the amalgamation of St. Sidwell United FC & Exeter United FC
Nickname: 'Grecians'
Ground: St. James Park, Exeter, EX4 6PX
Ground Capacity: 8,977
Seating Capacity: 3,806
Record Attendance: 20,984 (4/3/31)

Pitch Size: 113 × 71 yards
Colours: Red and White striped shirts, Black shorts
Telephone Nº: (01392) 411243
Ticket Office: (01392) 411243
Fax Number: (01392) 413959
Web Site: www.exetercityfc.co.uk

GENERAL INFORMATION
Car Parking: King William Street
Coach Parking: Paris Street Bus Station
Nearest Railway Station: Exeter St. James Park (adjacent)
Nearest Bus Station: Paris Street Bus Station
Club Shop: At the ground
Opening Times: Weekdays 10.00am to 5.00pm and Matchdays from 10.00am until kick-off
Telephone Nº: (01392) 411243
Police Telephone Nº: (0990) 700400

GROUND INFORMATION
Away Supporters' Entrances & Sections:
St. James Road turnstiles for standing in the St. James Road End or Well Street for seating in the Stagecoach Family Stand

ADMISSION INFO (2006/2007 PRICES)
Adult Standing: £13.00
Adult Seating: £15.00 – £16.00
Senior Citizen/Child Standing: £6.00 – £8.00
Senior Citizen/Child Seating: £6.00 – £10.00
Programme Price: £2.70

DISABLED INFORMATION
Wheelchairs: Accommodated in the Doble Stand and Cliff Bastin Stand
Helpers: One helper admitted per wheelchair
Prices: Free of charge for disabled. Normal prices for helpers
Disabled Toilets: Available by the Cliff Bastin Stand
Contact: (01392) 411243   (Bookings are necessary)

Travelling Supporters' Information:
Routes: From the North: Exit the M5 at Junction 30 and follow signs to the City Centre along Sidmouth Road and onto Heavitree Road. Take the 4th exit at the roundabout into Western Way and the 2nd exit into Tiverton Road then next left into St. James Road; From the East: Take the A30 into Heavitree Road (then as from the North); From the South & West: Take the A38 and follow City Centre signs into Western Way, then take the third exit at the roundabout into St. James Road.
Note: This ground is very difficult to find being in a residential area on the side of a hill without prominent floodlights.

FOREST GREEN ROVERS FC

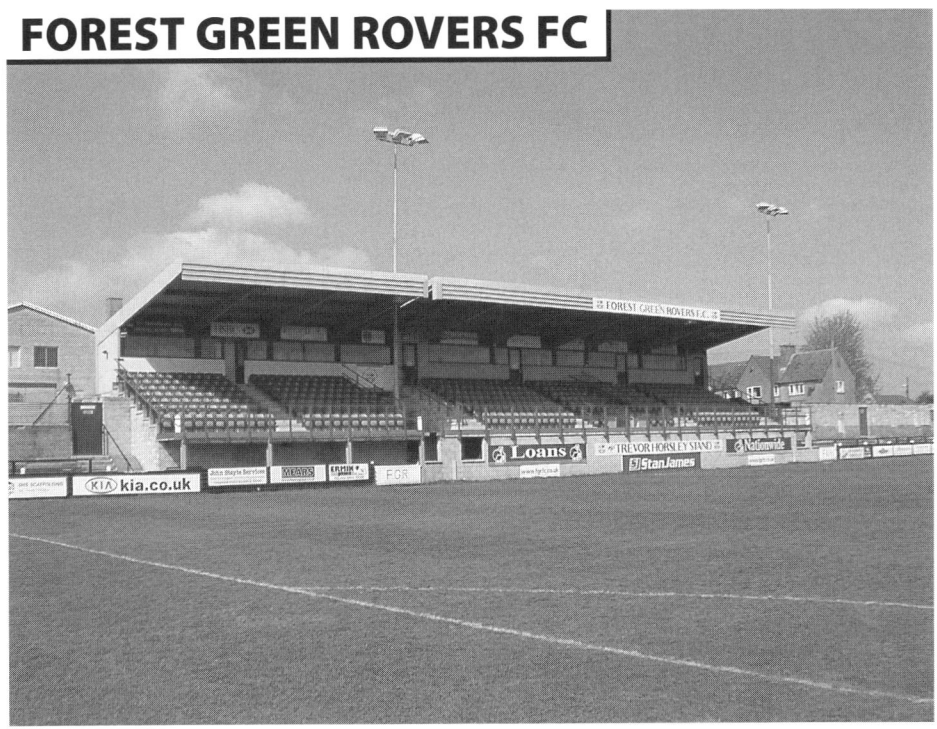

Founded: 1890
Former Names: Stroud FC
Nickname: 'The Rovers'
Ground: The Lawn, Nympsfield Road, Forest Green, Nailsworth, Gloucestershire GL6 0ET
Record Attendance: 3,002 (18/4/99)
Pitch Size: 110 × 70 yards

Colours: Black and White striped shirts, Black shorts
Telephone Nº: (01453) 834860
Fax Number: (01453) 835291
Ground Capacity: 5,141
Seating Capacity: 526
Web site: www.fgrfc.co.uk

GENERAL INFORMATION
Supporters Club: Andrew Whiting, c/o Club
Telephone Nº: (07979) 635087
Car Parking: At the ground
Coach Parking: At the ground
Nearest Railway Station: Stroud
Nearest Bus Station: Nailsworth
Club Shop: At the ground
Opening Times: Matchdays only
Telephone Nº: (07979) 635087
Police Telephone Nº: (01452) 521201

GROUND INFORMATION
Away Supporters' Entrances & Sections:
No usual segregation

ADMISSION INFO (2006/2007 PRICES)
Adult Standing: £11.00
Adult Seating: £13.00
Senior Citizen Standing: £7.00
Senior Citizen Seating: £9.00
Child Standing: £5.00
Child Seating: £7.00
Junior Greens: £2.00 – £3.00
Programme Price: £2.50

DISABLED INFORMATION
Wheelchairs: Accommodated in the Main Stand
Helpers: Admitted
Prices: Normal prices for the disabled. Free for helpers
Disabled Toilets: Yes
Contact: (01453) 834860 (Bookings necessary at least 72 hours in advance)

Travelling Supporters' Information:
Routes: The ground is located 4 miles south of Stroud on the A46 to Bath. Upon entering Nailsworth, turn into Spring Hill at the mini-roundabout and the ground is approximately ½ mile up the hill on the left.

GRAVESEND & NORTHFLEET FC

Founded: 1946
Former Names: Formed by the amalgamation of Gravesend United FC & Northfleet United FC
Nickname: 'The Fleet'
Ground: Stonebridge Road, Northfleet, Gravesend, Kent DA11 9GN
Record Attendance: 12,063 (1963)

Colours: Reds shirts with White shorts
Telephone Nº: (01474) 533796
Fax Number: (01474) 324754
Pitch Size: 112 × 72 yards
Ground Capacity: 4,200
Seating Capacity: 600
Web site: www.gnfc.co.uk

GENERAL INFORMATION
Supporters Club: c/o Club
Telephone Nº: (01474) 533796
Car Parking: At the ground and also street parking
Coach Parking: At the ground
Nearest Railway Station: Northfleet (5 minutes walk)
Nearest Bus Station: Bus Stop outside the ground
Club Shop: At the ground
Opening Times: Matchdays only
Telephone Nº: (01474) 533796
Police Telephone Nº: (01474) 564346

GROUND INFORMATION
Away Supporters' Entrances & Sections:
Only some games are segregated – contact club for details

ADMISSION INFO (2006/2007 PRICES)
Adult Standing: £12.00
Adult Seating: £14.00
Senior Citizen/Child Standing: £6.00
Senior Citizen/Child Seating: £7.00
Programme Price: £2.50

DISABLED INFORMATION
Wheelchairs: 6 spaces are available in the Disabled Area in front of the Main Stand
Helpers: Admitted free of charge
Prices: Please phone the club for information
Disabled Toilets: Available in the Main Stand
Contact: (01474) 533796 (Bookings are necessary)

Travelling Supporters' Information:
Routes: Take the A2 to the Northfleet/Southfleet exit and follow signs for Northfleet (B262). Go straight on at the first roundabout then take the 2nd exit at the 2nd roundabout into Thames Way and follow the football signs for the ground.

GRAYS ATHLETIC FC

Founded: 1890
Former Names: None
Nickname: 'The Blues'
Ground: The New Recreation Ground, Bridge Road, Grays, Essex   RM17 6BZ
Record Attendance: 9,500 (1959)
Pitch Size: 110 × 71 yards

Colours: Sky Blue shirts and shorts
Telephone Nº: (01375) 377753
Fax Number: (01375) 391649
Ground Capacity: 4,000
Seating Capacity: 900
Web site: www.graysathletic.co.uk

GENERAL INFORMATION

Supporters Club: None
Telephone Nº: –
Car Parking: Town Centre Car Parks close to the ground
Coach Parking: Car Parks close to the ground
Nearest Railway Station: Grays
Nearest Bus Station: Grays
Club Shop: At the ground
Opening Times: Matchdays only
Telephone Nº: (01375) 377753
Police Telephone Nº: (01375) 391212

GROUND INFORMATION

Away Supporters' Entrances & Sections:
Bradbourne Road entrances and accommodation

ADMISSION INFO (2006/2007 PRICES)

Adult Standing: £12.00
Adult Seating: £12.00
Concessionary Standing: £7.00
Concessionary Seating: £7.00
Programme Price: £2.50

DISABLED INFORMATION

Wheelchairs: Accommodated in the Main Stand
Helpers: One admitted free of charge per disabled fan
Prices: Please phone the club for information
Disabled Toilets: One available
Contact: (01375) 391649

Travelling Supporters' Information:
Routes: Exit the M25 at Junction 30 and take the A13 towards Southend. At the Grays exit, follow signs to the town centre. Upon reaching the one-way system, keep to the left and continue uphill for about ½ miles before turning right into Bridge Road. The ground is then on the right.

HALIFAX TOWN FC

Founded: 1911
Nickname: 'Shaymen'
Ground: Shay Ground, Shay Syke, Halifax HX1 2YS
Ground Capacity: 11,445
Seating Capacity: 2,912
Record Attendance: 36,885 (14/2/53)
Pitch Size: 110 × 75 yards

Colours: Blue and White shirts with Blue shorts
Telephone Nº: (01422) 341222
Ticket Office: (01422) 341222
Fax Number: (01422) 349487
Web Site: www.halifaxafc.co.uk
E-mail: theshay@halifaxafc.co.uk

GENERAL INFORMATION
Car Parking: Shaw Hill Car Park (Nearby)
Coach Parking: Shaw Hill
Nearest Railway Station: Halifax (10 minutes walk)
Nearest Bus Station: Halifax (20 minutes walk)
Club Shop: At the ground
Opening Times: Please phone for details
Telephone Nº: (0870) 411-7111

GROUND INFORMATION
Away Supporters' Entrances & Sections:
North Stand

ADMISSION INFO (2006/2007 PRICES)
Adult Standing: £13.00
Adult Seating: £13.00
Under-16s/Senior Citizen Standing: £6.00
Under-16s/Senior Citizen Seating: £6.00
Under-12s Standing/Seating: £3.00
Programme Price: £2.50

DISABLED INFORMATION
Wheelchairs: 10 spaces available in the disabled section,
12 spaces available on the new North Terrace
Facilities for the visually impaired may be available.
Helpers: One admitted free with each paying disabled fan
Prices: Normal prices apply for the disabled.
Disabled Toilets: In the Main Stand and the new North and
South Terraces
Contact: (01422) 434212 (Bookings are not necessary)

Travelling Supporters' Information:
Routes: From the North: Take the A629 to Halifax Town Centre. Take the 2nd exit at the roundabout into Broad Street and follow signs for Huddersfield (A629) into Skircoat Road; From the South, East and West: Exit the M62 at Junction 24 and follow Halifax (A629) signs for the Town Centre into Skircoat Road then Shaw Hill for ground.

KIDDERMINSTER HARRIERS FC

Founded: 1886
Nickname: 'Harriers'
Ground: Aggborough, Hoo Road, Kidderminster, Worcestershire DY10 1NB
Ground Capacity: 6,444
Seating Capacity: 3,143
Record Attendance: 9,155 (1948)

Pitch Size: 110 × 72 yards
Colours: Red shirts with Black shorts
Telephone Nº: (01562) 823931
Fax Number: (01562) 827329
Web Site: www.harriers.co.uk

GENERAL INFORMATION

Car Parking: At the ground
Coach Parking: As directed
Nearest Railway Station: Kidderminster
Nearest Bus Station: Kidderminster Town Centre
Club Shop: At the ground
Opening Times: Weekdays and First Team Matchdays 9.00am to 5.00pm
Telephone Nº: (01562) 823931
Police Telephone Nº: –

GROUND INFORMATION

Away Supporters' Entrances & Sections:
John Smiths Stand Entrance D and South Terrace Entrance E

ADMISSION INFO (2006/2007 PRICES)

Adult Standing: £13.00
Adult Seating: £16.00
Senior Citizen Standing: £8.00   **Under-16s**: £5.00
Concessionary Seating: £11.00
Note: Under-8s are admitted free with a paying adult
Programme Price: £2.50

DISABLED INFORMATION

Wheelchairs: Accommodated at the front of the John Smiths Stand
Helpers: Admitted
Prices: £10.00 for each disabled fan plus one helper
Disabled Toilets: Available by the disabled area
Contact: (01562) 823931   (Bookings are not necessary)

Travelling Supporters' Information:
Routes: Exit the M5 at Junction 3 and follow the A456 to Kidderminster. The ground is situated close by the Severn Valley Railway Station so follow the brown Steam Train signs and turn into Hoo Road about 200 yards downhill of the station. Follow the road along for ¼ mile and the ground is on the left.

MORECAMBE FC

Founded: 1920
Former Names: None
Nickname: 'Shrimps'
Ground: Christie Park, Lancaster Road, Morecambe, LA4 5TJ
Record Attendance: 9,324 (1962)
Pitch Size: 118 × 76 yards

Colours: Red shirts with White shorts
Telephone Nº: (01524) 411797
Daytime Phone Nº: (01524) 411797
Fax Number: (01524) 832230
Ground Capacity: 6,300
Seating Capacity: 1,200
Web site: www.morecambefc.com

GENERAL INFORMATION

Supporters Club: c/o Club
Telephone Nº: –
Car Parking: At the ground
Coach Parking: At the ground
Nearest Railway Station: Morecambe Central (½ mile)
Nearest Bus Station: Morecambe
Club Shop: At the ground
Opening Times: Weekdays & Matchdays 9.00am to 5.00pm
Telephone Nº: (01524) 411797
Police Telephone Nº: (01524) 411534

GROUND INFORMATION

Away Supporters' Entrances & Sections:
Entrances at the corner of the South Terrace and Lancaster Road for South Terrace accommodation (when segregated)

ADMISSION INFO (2006/2007 PRICES)

Adult Standing: £12.00
Adult Seating: £13.00
Child Standing: £4.00
Child Seating: £5.00
Senior Citizen Standing: £9.00
Senior Citizen Seating: £10.00
Programme Price: £2.50

DISABLED INFORMATION

Wheelchairs: 18 spaces available in the Disabled Stand and 20 spaces are available in the North Stand
Helpers: Admitted
Prices: Concessionary prices are charged
Disabled Toilets: Available in the North Stand
Contact: (01524) 411797 (Bookings are preferred)

Travelling Supporters' Information:
Routes: Exit the M6 at Junction 34. Then take the A683 west in Lancaster and pick up the A589 to Morecambe. At the 2nd roundabout on the outskirts of Morecambe, take the 2nd exit into Lancaster Road and the ground is on the left, approximately 800 yards.

NORTHWICH VICTORIA FC

Founded: 1874
Former Names: None
Nickname: 'The Vics' 'The Greens' 'The Trickies'
Ground: Victoria Stadium, Wincham Avenue,
Wincham, Northwich   CW9 6GB
Record Attendance: –
Pitch Size: 112 × 74 yards

Colours: Green & White hooped shirts, White shorts
Office Telephone Nº: (01606) 41555
Fax Number: (01606) 41565
Ground Capacity: 5,294
Seating Capacity: 1,294
Web site: www.northwichvics.co.uk

GENERAL INFORMATION
Supporters Club: Dave Thomas, c/o Club
Telephone Nº: (01606) 41555
Car Parking: Ample parking spaces available at the ground
Coach Parking: At the ground
Nearest Railway Station: Northwich (2½ miles)
Nearest Bus Station: Northwich (2½ miles)
Club Shop: At the ground
Opening Times: Weekdays & Matchdays 10.00am–4.00pm
Telephone Nº: (01606) 41555
Police Telephone Nº: (01606) 48000

GROUND INFORMATION
Away Supporters' Entrances & Sections: Not specified

ADMISSION INFO (2006/2007 PRICES)
Adult Standing: £12.00
Adult Seating: £14.00
Senior Citizen Standing: £10.00
Senior Citizen Seating: £12.00
Under-16s Standing: £5.00
Under-16s Seating: £7.00
Under-12s Standing/Seating: £2.50
Programme Price: £2.00

DISABLED INFORMATION
Wheelchairs: 46 spaces are available in total
Helpers: Admitted
Prices: Free for the disabled. Helpers pay normal prices
Disabled Toilets: Yes
Contact: (01606) 41555   (Please phone to book)

Travelling Supporters' Information:
Routes: Exit the M6 at Junction 19 and take the A556 towards Northwich. After 3 miles turn right onto the A559 following signs for Warrington. Turn left after Marston opposite the Black Greyhound Inn then left into Wincham Avenue after 200 yards. Alternative Route: Exit the M56 at Junction 10 and take the A559 to the Black Greyhound Inn then turn right. Then as above

OXFORD UNITED FC

Founded: 1893 (**Entered League**: 1962)
Former Names: Headington United FC (1893-1960)
Nickname: 'U's'
Ground: Kassam Stadium, Grenoble Road, Oxford, OX4 4XP
Ground Capacity: 12,500 (All seats)
Record Attendance: 22,730 (At the Manor Ground)

Pitch Size: 115 × 71 yards
Colours: Yellow shirts with Navy Blue shorts
Telephone Nº: (01865) 337500
Ticket Office: (01865) 337533
Fax Number: (01865) 337555
Web Site: www.oufc.co.uk

GENERAL INFORMATION
Car Parking: 2,000 free spaces available at the ground
Coach Parking: At the ground
Nearest Railway Station: Oxford (4 miles)
Nearest Bus Station: Oxford
Club Shop: At the ground
Opening Times: Monday to Friday 10.00 – 5.00pm; Saturdays 10am – 4.00pm (Matchdays until 2.45pm)
Telephone Nº: (01865) 335310
Police Telephone Nº: (01865) 749909

GROUND INFORMATION
Away Supporters' Entrances & Sections:
North Stand turnstiles for North Stand accommodation. Ticket office for away supporters is adjacent

ADMISSION INFO (2006/2007 PRICES)
Adult Seating: £16.00 – £19.50
Under-16s Seating: £5.50 – £13.00
Senior Citizen Seating: £8.50 – £13.00
Note: Discounts are available for advance bookings
Programme Price: £2.50

DISABLED INFORMATION
Wheelchairs: Accommodated in areas in the North, East and South Stands
Helpers: One helper admitted per disabled person
Prices: Normal prices for the disabled. One helper admitted free of charge per disabled fan if required
Disabled Toilets: Available
Commentaries are available for the visually impaired
Contact: (01865) 337533   (Bookings are not necessary)

Travelling Supporters' Information:
Routes: From the Oxford Ring Road take the A423 towards Henley and Reading then turn left after ½ mile following signs for the Oxford Science Park. Bear left and go straight on at two roundabouts then the Stadium is on the left in Grenoble Road. The Kassam Stadium is clearly signposted on all major roads in Oxford.

RUSHDEN & DIAMONDS FC

Founded: 1992   (**Entered League**: 2001)
Former Names: Formed by the amalgamation of
Rushden Town FC and Irthlingborough Diamonds FC
Nickname: 'Diamonds'
Ground: Nene Park, Diamond Way, Irthlingborough,
Northants   NN9 5QF
Ground Capacity: 6,441
Seating Capacity: 4,641

Record Attendance: 6,431· (1999)
Pitch Size: 111 × 74 yards
Colours: Red shirts, shorts and socks
Telephone Nº: (01933) 652000
Fax Number: (01933) 652606
Web Site: www.thediamondsfc.com

GENERAL INFORMATION
Car Parking: At the ground (£2.00 charge)
Coach Parking: At the ground (£10.00 charge)
Nearest Railway Station: Wellingborough (5 miles)
Nearest Bus Station: Wellingborough
Club Shop: Yes – at the 'Doc' Shop
Opening Times: Monday–Friday 9.30am–5.30pm (7.00pm
on Wednesdays); Saturday matchdays 10.00am to 3.00pm
and 4.45pm–5.30pm; Other Saturdays 9.00am–1.00pm
Telephone Nº: (01933) 652000
Police Telephone Nº: (01933) 440333

GROUND INFORMATION
Away Supporters' Entrances & Sections:
Airwair Stand

ADMISSION INFO (2006/2007 PRICES)
Adult Standing: £12.00 (Home fans only)
Adult Seating: £15.00
Concessionary Standing: £7.00
Concessionary Seating: £10.00
Under-16s Standing/Seating: £4.00
Note: Under-8s are admitted free with a paying adult
Programme Price: £2.50

DISABLED INFORMATION
Wheelchairs: Accommodated around the ground
Helpers: Admitted
Prices: £7.00 – £10.00 for the disabled with helpers
admitted free of charge
Disabled Toilets: Available around the ground
Contact: (01933) 652936   (Bookings are preferred)

Travelling Supporters' Information:
Routes: The ground is located on the A6 about 350 yards north of the junction with the A45 (over the bridge). This is
approximately 6 miles south of the A14.

SOUTHPORT FC

Founded: 1881
Former Names: Southport Vulcan FC, Southport Central FC
Nickname: 'The Sandgrounders'
Ground: Haig Avenue, Southport, Merseyside, PR8 6JZ
Record Attendance: 20,010 (1932)
Pitch Size: 110 × 77 yards

Colours: Yellow shirts and shorts
Telephone Nº: (01704) 533422
Fax Number: (01704) 533455
Ground Capacity: 6,001
Seating Capacity: 1,640
Web site: www.southportfc.net

GENERAL INFORMATION

Supporters Club: Grandstand Club
Telephone Nº: (01704) 530182
Car Parking: Street parking
Coach Parking: Adjacent to the ground
Nearest Railway Station: Southport (1½ miles)
Nearest Bus Station: Southport Town Centre
Club Shop: At the ground
Opening Times: Matchdays from 1.30pm (or 6.30pm for evening matches); Fridays 4.30pm to 6.30pm
Telephone Nº: (01704) 533422
Police Telephone Nº: (0151) 709-6010

GROUND INFORMATION

Away Supporters' Entrances & Sections: Blowick End entrances

ADMISSION INFO (2006/2007 PRICES)

Adult Standing: £11.00
Adult Seating: £12.50
Child/Senior Citizen Standing: £7.50
Child/Senior Citizen Seating: £8.50
Programme Price: £2.50

DISABLED INFORMATION

Wheelchairs: Accommodated in front of the Grandstand
Helpers: Admitted
Prices: Concessionary prices charged for the disabled. Helpers are admitted free of charge
Disabled Toilets: Available at the Blowick End of the Grandstand
Contact: (01704) 533422 (Bookings are not necessary)

Travelling Supporters' Information:
Routes: Exit the M58 at Junction 3 and take the A570 to Southport. At the major roundabout (McDonalds/Tesco) go straight on into Scarisbrick New Road, pass over the brook and turn right into Haig Avenue at the traffic lights. The ground is then on the right-hand side.

STAFFORD RANGERS FC

Founded: 1876
Former Names: None
Nickname: 'The Boro'
Ground: Marston Road, Stafford   ST16 3BX
Record Attendance: 8,523 (4/1/75)
Pitch Size: 112 × 75 yards

Colours: Black and White striped shirts, Black shorts
Telephone Nº: (01785) 602430
Social Club Nº: (01785) 602432
Ground Capacity: 3,472
Seating Capacity: 532
Web site: www.staffordrangers.co.uk

GENERAL INFORMATION
Supporters Club: c/o Social Club
Telephone Nº: (01785) 602432
Car Parking: At the ground
Coach Parking: Astonfields Road
Nearest Railway Station: Stafford (1½ miles)
Nearest Bus Station: Stafford
Club Shop: At the ground
Opening Times: Matchdays only
Telephone Nº: (01785) 602430
Police Telephone Nº: (01785) 258151

GROUND INFORMATION
Away Supporters' Entrances & Sections:
Lotus End

ADMISSION INFO (2006/2007 PRICES)
Adult Standing: £12.00
Adult Seating: £14.00
Concessionary Standing: £8.00
Concessionary Seating: £10.00
Children under the age of 12 are admitted for £2.00 when accompanied by a paying adult
Programme Price: £2.00

DISABLED INFORMATION
Wheelchairs: Accommodated at Marston Road End
Helpers: Admitted
Prices: Concessionary prices for the disabled. Normal prices for helpers
Disabled Toilets: Available
Contact: (01785) 602430   (Bookings are not necessary)

Travelling Supporters' Information:
Routes: Exit the M6 at Junction 14 and take the slip road signposted 'Stone/Stafford'. Continue to traffic island and go straight across then take the 3rd exit on the right into Common Road, signposted 'Common Road/Aston Fields Industrial Estate'. Follow the road to the bridge and bear left over the bridge. The ground is on the right.

ST. ALBANS CITY FC

Founded: 1908
Former Names: None
Nickname: 'The Saints'
Ground: Clarence Park, York Road, St. Albans, Hertfordshire   AL1 4PL
Record Attendance: 9,757 (27/2/26)
Pitch Size: 110 × 80 yards

Colours: Yellow shirts with Blue trim, Yellow shorts
Telephone Nº: (01727) 864296
Fax Number: (01727) 866235
Ground Capacity: 5,007
Seating Capacity: 667
Web site: www.sacfc.co.uk

GENERAL INFORMATION
Supporters Club: Ian Rogers, c/o Club
Telephone Nº: –
Car Parking: Street parking
Coach Parking: In Clarence Park
Nearest Railway Station: St. Albans City (200 yds)
Nearest Bus Station: City Centre (short walk)
Club Shop: At the ground
Opening Times: Matchdays only
Telephone Nº: (01727) 864296
Police Telephone Nº: (01727) 276122

GROUND INFORMATION
Away Supporters' Entrances & Sections:
Hatfield Road End when matches are segregated

ADMISSION INFO (2006/2007 PRICES)
Adult Standing: £12.00
Adult Seating: £14.00
Under-12s Standing: £5.00   **OAP/Under-16s**: £8.00
Under-12s Seating: £6.00   **OAP/Under-16s**: £9.00
Programme Price: £2.00

DISABLED INFORMATION
Wheelchairs: Accommodated
Helpers: One admitted per disabled supporter
Prices: Free for the disabled, concessionary prices for the helpers
Disabled Toilets: Available inside new Building at the York Road End
Contact: (01727) 864296   (Bookings are not necessary)

Travelling Supporters' Information:
Routes: Take the M1 or M10 to the A405 North Orbital Road and at the roundabout at the start of the M10, go north on the A5183 (Watling Street). Turn right along St. Stephen's Hill and carry along into St. Albans. Continue up Holywell Hill, go through two sets of traffic lights and at the end of St. Peter's Street, take a right turn at the roundabout into Hatfield Road. Follow over the mini-roundabouts and at the second set of traffic lights turn left into Clarence Road and the ground is on the left. Park in Clarence Road and enter the ground via the Park or in York Road and use the entrance by the footbridge.

STEVENAGE BOROUGH FC

Founded: 1976
Former Names: None
Nickname: 'Boro'
Ground: Stevenage Stadium, Broadhall Way, Stevenage, Hertfordshire SG2 8RH
Record Attendance: 8,040 (25/1/98)
Pitch Size: 110 × 70 yards

Colours: Red, Black and White shirts with Black shorts
Telephone Nº: (01438) 223223
Daytime Phone Nº: (01438) 223223
Fax Number: (01438) 743666
Ground Capacity: 7,104
Seating Capacity: 3,404
Web site: www.stevenageborofc.com

GENERAL INFORMATION

Supporters Club: Mervyn Stoke Geddis, 21 Woodland Way, Stevenage
Telephone Nº: (01438) 313236
Car Parking: Fairlands Show Ground (opposite)
Coach Parking: At the ground
Nearest Railway Station: Stevenage (1 mile)
Nearest Bus Station: Stevenage
Club Shop: At the ground
Opening Times: Tuesday to Thursday and matchdays 10.00am to 5.00pm
Telephone Nº: 0870 811-2494
Police Telephone Nº: (01438) 757000

GROUND INFORMATION

Away Supporters' Entrances & Sections:
South Terrace entrances and accommodation

ADMISSION INFO (2006/2007 PRICES)

Adult Standing: £11.00
Adult Seating: £14.00
Senior Citizen/Child Standing: £7.00 – £9.00
Senior Citizen/Child Seating: £11.00
Programme Price: £2.00

DISABLED INFORMATION

Wheelchairs: 10 spaces available in total by the North Terrace
Helpers: Admitted
Prices: £9.00 for the disabled. Free of charge for helpers
Disabled Toilets: Yes
Contact: (01438) 223223 (Bookings are necessary)

Travelling Supporters' Information:
Routes: Exit the A1(M) at Junction 7 and take the B197. The ground is on the right at the 2nd roundabout.
Bus Routes: SB4 and SB5

TAMWORTH FC

Founded: 1933
Former Names: None
Nickname: 'The Lambs'
Ground: The Lamb Ground, Kettlebrook, Tamworth, B77 1AA
Record Attendance: 4,920 (3/4/48)
Pitch Size: 110 × 73 yards

Colours: Red shirts and shorts
Telephone Nº: (01827) 65798
Daytime Phone Nº: (01827) 65798
Fax Number: (01827) 62236
Ground Capacity: 4,118
Seating Capacity: 520
Web site: www.thelambs.co.uk

GENERAL INFORMATION

Supporters Club: Dave Clayton, c/o Club
Telephone Nº: (0781) 5046899
Car Parking: 200 spaces available at the ground – £1.00 per car or £10.00 per coach
Coach Parking: At the ground
Nearest Railway Station: Tamworth (½ mile)
Nearest Bus Station: Tamworth (½ mile)
Club Shop: At the ground
Opening Times: Weekdays & Matchdays 10.00am – 4.00pm
Telephone Nº: (01827) 65798
Police Telephone Nº: (01827) 61001

GROUND INFORMATION

Away Supporters' Entrances & Sections:
Gates 1 and 2 for Terracing, Gate 2A for seating

ADMISSION INFO (2006/2007 PRICES)

Adult Standing: £11.00
Adult Seating: £13.00
Child/Senior Citizen Standing: £6.00
Child/Senior Citizen Seating: £9.00
Programme Price: £2.00

DISABLED INFORMATION

Wheelchairs: Accommodated
Helpers: Admitted
Prices: Normal prices apply for Wheelchair disabled. Helpers are charged concessionary rates
Disabled Toilets: Yes
Contact: (01827) 65798   (Bookings are advisable)

Travelling Supporters' Information:
Routes: Exit the M42 at Junction 10 and take the A5/A51 to the town centre following signs for Town Centre/Snowdome. The follow signs for Kettlebrook and the ground is in Kettlebrook Road, 50 yards from the traffic island by the Railway Viaduct and the Snowdome. The ground is signposted from all major roads.

WEYMOUTH FC

Founded: 1890
Former Names: None
Nickname: 'Terras'
Ground: Wessex Stadium, Radipole Lane, Weymouth, Dorset   DT4 9XJ
Record Attendance: 6,500   (14th November 2005)
Pitch Size: 115 × 74 yards

Colours: Shirts are Claret and Sky Blue, Claret shorts
Telephone N°: (01305) 785558
Fax Number: (01305) 766658
Ground Capacity: 6,500
Seating Capacity: 800
Web site: www.theterras.co.uk

GENERAL INFORMATION
Supporters Club: Nigel Beckett, c/o Club
Telephone N°: (01305) 785558
Car Parking: 200 spaces available at the ground
Coach Parking: At the ground
Nearest Railway Station: Weymouth (2 miles)
Nearest Bus Station: Weymouth Town Centre
Club Shop: At the ground
Opening Times: Matchdays only
Telephone N°: –
Police Telephone N°: (01305) 251212

GROUND INFORMATION
Away Supporters' Entrances & Sections:
Visitors End turnstiles and accommodation when segregation is used

ADMISSION INFO (2006/2007 PRICES)
Adult Standing: £13.00
Adult Seating: £15.00
Senior Citizen Standing: £8.00
Senior Citizen Seating: £10.00
Under-15s Standing: £5.00
Under-15s Seating: £7.00
Programme Price: £2.00

DISABLED INFORMATION
Wheelchairs: Accommodated
Helpers: Admitted
Prices: Normal prices apply for the disabled. Free for helpers
Disabled Toilets: Yes
Contact: (01305) 785558   (Bookings are not necessary)

Travelling Supporters' Information:
Routes: Take the A354 from Dorchester to Weymouth and turn right at the first roundabout to the town centre. Take the 3rd exit at the next roundabout and follow signs for the ground which is about ½ mile on the right.

WOKING FC

Founded: 1889
Former Names: None
Nickname: 'Cardinals'
Ground: Kingfield Stadium, Kingfield, Woking, Surrey   GU22 9AA
Record Attendance: 6,000 (1997)
Pitch Size: 109 × 76 yards

Colours: Shirts are Red & White halves, Black shorts
Telephone N°: (01483) 772470
Daytime Phone N°: (01483) 772470
Fax Number: (01483) 888423
Ground Capacity: 6,161
Seating Capacity: 2,511
Web site: www.wokingfc.co.uk

GENERAL INFORMATION

Supporters Club: Mr. G. Burnett (Secretary), c/o Club
Telephone N°: (01483) 772470
Car Parking: Limited parking at the ground
Coach Parking: At or opposite the ground
Nearest Railway Station: Woking (1 mile)
Nearest Bus Station: Woking
Club Shop: At the ground
Opening Times: Weekdays and Matchdays
Telephone N°: (01483) 772470
Police Telephone N°: (01483) 761991

GROUND INFORMATION

Away Supporters' Entrances & Sections:
Kingfield Road when segregation is in force

ADMISSION INFO (2006/2007 PRICES)

Adult Standing: £12.00
Adult Seating: £15.00
Child Standing: £5.00
Child Seating: £6.00
Senior Citizen Standing: £10.00
Senior Citizen Seating: £11.00
Programme Price: £2.50

DISABLED INFORMATION

Wheelchairs: 8 spaces in the Leslie Gosden Stand and 8 spaces in front of the Family Stand
Helpers: Admitted
Prices: One wheelchair and helper for £11.00
Disabled Toilets: Yes – in the Leslie Gosden Stand and Family Stand area
Contact: (01483) 772470   (Bookings are necessary)

Travelling Supporters' Information:
Routes: Exit the M25 at Junction 10 and follow the A3 towards Guildford. Leave at the next junction onto the B2215 through Ripley and join the A247 to Woking. Alternatively, exit the M25 at Junction 11 and follow the A320 to Woking Town Centre. The ground is on the outskirts of Woking – follow signs on the A320 and A247.

YORK CITY FC

Founded: 1922
Nickname: 'Minstermen'
Ground: Kit Kat Crescent, York   YO30 7AQ
Ground Capacity: 9,496
Seating Capacity: 3,509
Record Attendance: 28,123 (5/3/38)
Pitch Size: 115 × 74 yards

Colours: Red shirts with White shorts
Telephone Nº: (0870) 7771922
Ticket Office: (0870) 7771922 Extension 1
Fax Number: (0870) 7741993
Web Site: www.ycfc.net

GENERAL INFORMATION
Car Parking: Street parking
Coach Parking: By Police direction
Nearest Railway Station: York (1 mile)
Nearest Bus Station: York
Club Shop: At the ground
Opening Times: Weekdays 10.30am – 2.30pm and Saturday Matchdays 1.00pm–3.00pm and 4.40pm–5.30pm
Telephone Nº: (0870) 7771922 Extension 4
Police Telephone Nº: (01904) 631321

GROUND INFORMATION
Away Supporters' Entrances & Sections:
Grosvenor Road turnstiles for Grosvenor Road End

ADMISSION INFO (2006/2007 PRICES)
Adult Standing: £13.00
Adult Seating: £14.00 – £16.00
Child Standing: £8.00
Child Seating: £5.00 – £10.00
Note: Concessions are available in the Family Stand
Programme Price: £2.50

DISABLED INFORMATION
Wheelchairs: 18 spaces in total for Home and Away fans in the disabled section, in front of the Social Club
Helpers: One helper admitted per disabled person
Prices: £14.00 for the disabled. Free of charge for helpers
Disabled Toilets: Available at entrance to the disabled area
Commentaries are available for the blind
Contact: (0870) 7771922 (Ext. 1) (Bookings not necessary)

Travelling Supporters' Information:
Routes: From the North: Take the A1 then the A59 following signs for York. Cross the railway bridge and turn left after 2 miles into Water End. Turn right at the end following City Centre signs for nearly ½ mile then turn left into Bootham Crescent; From the South: Take the A64 and turn left after Buckles Inn onto the Outer Ring Road. Turn right onto the A19, follow City Centre signs for 1½ miles then turn left into Bootham Crescent; From the East: Take the Outer Ring Road turning left onto the A19. Then as from the South; From the West: Take the Outer Ring Road turning right onto the A19. Then as from the South.

THE NATIONWIDE FOOTBALL CONFERENCE NORTH CLUBS

Address
Riverside House, 14B High Street,
Crayford, Kent   DA1 4HG

Phone (01322) 411021   **Fax** (01322) 411022

Clubs for the 2006/2007 Season

ALFRETON TOWN FC

Founded: 1959
Former Names: None
Nickname: 'Reds'
Ground: The Impact Arena, North Street, Alfreton, Derbyshire
Record Attendance: 5,023 vs Matlock Town (1960)
Pitch Size: 110 × 75 yards

Colours: Red shirts and shorts
Telephone Nº: (01773) 830277
Fax Number: (01773) 836164
Ground Capacity: 5,000
Seating Capacity: 1,600
Web site: www.alfretontownfc.com

GENERAL INFORMATION
Supporters Club: Mark Thorpe, c/o Social Club
Telephone Nº: (01773) 836251
Car Parking: At the ground
Coach Parking: At the ground
Nearest Railway Station: Alfreton (½ mile)
Nearest Bus Station: Alfreton (5 minutes walk)
Club Shop: At the ground
Opening Times: Matchdays (including Youth & Reserves)
Telephone Nº: (01773) 830277
Police Telephone Nº: (01773) 570100

GROUND INFORMATION
Away Supporters' Entrances & Sections:
No usual segregation

ADMISSION INFO (2006/2007 PRICES)
Adult Standing: £9.00
Adult Seating: £9.00
Senior Citizen/Junior Standing: £4.50
Senior Citizen/Junior Seating: £4.50
Programme Price: £2.00

DISABLED INFORMATION
Wheelchairs: Accommodated at the front of the Stand
Helpers: Admitted
Prices: Please phone the club for information
Disabled Toilets: Available in the Executive Bar
Contact: (01773) 830277 (Bookings are not necessary)

Travelling Supporters' Information:
Routes: Exit the M1 at Junction 28 and take the A38 signposted for Derby. After 2 miles take the sliproad onto the B600 then go right at the main road towards the town centre. After ½ mile turn left down North Street and the ground is on the right after 200 yards.

BARROW FC

Founded: 1901	**Colours**: Blue and White shirts with Blue shorts
Former Names: None	**Matchday Telephone Nº**: (01229) 820346
Nickname: 'Bluebirds'	**Weekday Telephone Nº**: (01229) 823061
Ground: Holker Street Stadium, Barrow-in-Furness, Cumbria LA14 5UQ	**Fax Number**: (01229) 820346/823061
Record Attendance: 16,874 (1954)	**Ground Capacity**: 5,000
Pitch Size: 110 × 75 yards	**Seating Capacity**: 1,064
	Web site: www.barrowafc.com

GENERAL INFORMATION

Supporters Club: Bill Ablitt, c/o Club
Telephone Nº: (01229) 471617
Car Parking: Street Parking, Popular Side Car Park and Soccer Bar Car Park
Coach Parking: Adjacent to the ground
Nearest Railway Station: Barrow Central (½ mile)
Nearest Bus Station: ½ mile
Club Shop: 60 Buccleuch Street, Barrow-in-Furness, LA14 1QG
Opening Times: Monday to Wednesday & Fridays 10.00am – 4.00pm, Saturdays 10.00am – 2.00pm
Telephone Nº: (01229) 823061 (weekdays)
Police Telephone Nº: (01229) 824532

GROUND INFORMATION

Away Supporters' Entrances & Sections:
West Terrace (not covered)

ADMISSION INFO (2006/2007 PRICES)

Adult Standing: £9.00
Adult Seating: £10.00
Concessionary Standing: £6.00
Concessionary Seating: £7.00
Under-14s: £3.00
Programme Price: £1.50

DISABLED INFORMATION

Wheelchairs: 6 spaces available in the Disabled Area
Helpers: Admitted
Prices: Normal prices apply
Disabled Toilets: Available
Contact: (01229) 820346   (Bookings are not necessary)

Travelling Supporters' Information:
Routes: Exit the M6 at Junction 36 and take the A590 through Ulverston. Using the bypass, follow signs for Barrow. After approximately 5 miles, turn left into Wilkie Road and the ground is on the left.

BLYTH SPARTANS FC

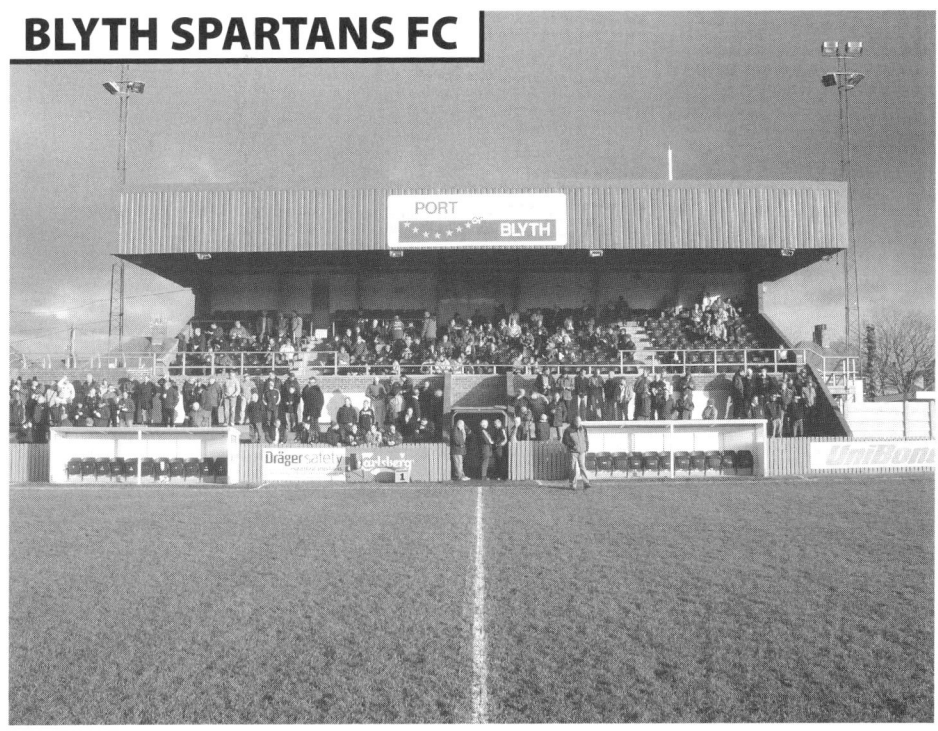

Founded: 1899
Former Names: None
Nickname: 'Spartans'
Ground: Croft Park, Blyth, Northumberland, NE24 3JE
Record Attendance: 10,186
Pitch Size: 110 × 70 yards

Colours: Green and White striped shirts, Black shorts
Telephone Nº: (01670) 352373 (Office)
Fax Number: (01670) 545592
Ground Capacity: 6,000
Seating Capacity: 339
Web site: www.blythspartansafc.co.uk

GENERAL INFORMATION
Supporters Club: Bobby Bell, c/o Club
Telephone Nº: (01670) 352373
Car Parking: At the ground
Coach Parking: At the ground
Nearest Railway Station: Newcastle
Nearest Bus Station: Blyth (5 minutes walk)
Club Shop: At the ground
Opening Times: Matchdays only
Telephone Nº: c/o (01670) 336379
Police Telephone Nº: (01661) 872555

GROUND INFORMATION
Away Supporters' Entrances & Sections:
No usual segregation

ADMISSION INFO (2006/2007 PRICES)
Adult Standing: £7.00
Adult Seating: £8.00
Child Standing: £4.00
Child Seating: £5.00
Programme Price: £1.30

DISABLED INFORMATION
Wheelchairs: Accommodated
Helpers: Please phone the club for information
Prices: Please phone the club for information
Disabled Toilets: Yes
Contact: (01670) 352373 (Bookings are necessary)

Travelling Supporters' Information:
Routes: Pass through the Tyne Tunnel and take the left lane for Morpeth (A19/A1). At the 2nd roundabout (after approximately 7 miles) take full right turn for the A189 (signposted Ashington). After 2 miles take the slip road (A1061 signposted Blyth). Follow signs for Blyth turning left at the caravan site. At the 2nd roundabout turn right and the ground is on the left.

DROYLSDEN FC

Founded: 1892
Former Names: None
Nickname: 'The Bloods'
Ground: Butchers Arms, Market Street, Droylsden, Manchester M43 7AY
Record Attendance: 5,400 (1973)
Pitch Size: 110 × 70 yards

Colours: Red shirts with Black shorts
Telephone Nº: (0161) 370-1426
Daytime Phone Nº: (0161) 370-1426
Fax Number: (0161) 370-8341
Ground Capacity: 3,500
Seating Capacity: 500
Web site: www.droylsdenfc.co.uk

GENERAL INFORMATION

Supporters Club: c/o Club
Telephone Nº: –
Car Parking: Street parking only
Coach Parking: At the ground
Nearest Railway Station: Manchester Piccadilly
Nearest Bus Station: Ashton
Club Shop: At the ground
Opening Times: Matchdays only
Telephone Nº: (0161) 370-1426
Police Telephone Nº: (0161) 330-8321

GROUND INFORMATION

Away Supporters' Entrances & Sections:
No usual segregation

ADMISSION INFO (2006/2007 PRICES)

Adult Standing: £10.00
Adult Seating: £10.00
Concessionary Standing: £6.00
Concessionary Seating: £6.00
Note: Under-14s are admitted free of charge
Programme Price: £2.00

DISABLED INFORMATION

Wheelchairs: Accommodated beside the Stand
Helpers: Yes
Prices: Normal prices apply for the disabled and helpers
Disabled Toilets: Available
Contact: (0161) 370-1426 (Bookings are not necessary)

Travelling Supporters' Information:
Routes: Take the Manchester Outer Ring Road M60 and exit at Junction 23. Join the A635 towards Manchester and after the retail park on the left, take the centre lane, then turn right at the traffic lights onto the A662 signposted for Droylsden. At the next traffic lights, turn right onto Market Street and after 150 yards go straight on at the traffic lights. The entrance to the ground is 75 yards on the left.

FARSLEY CELTIC FC

Founded: 1908
Former Names: None
Nickname: 'Villagers'
Ground: Throstle Nest, Newlands, Farsley, Leeds, LS28 5BE
Record Attendance: 2,462 (2001)
Pitch Size: 110 × 67 yards

Colours: Blue shirts and shorts
Telephone Nº: (0113) 255-7292
Fax Number: (0113) 256-1517
Ground Capacity: 4,000
Seating Capacity: 300
Web site: www.farsleyceltic.co.uk

GENERAL INFORMATION
Car Parking: Available at the ground
Coach Parking: Available at the ground
Nearest Railway Station: New Pudsey (1 mile)
Nearest Bus Station: Pudsey (1 mile)
Club Shop: At the ground
Opening Times: Weekday evenings 6.00pm – 11.00pm and weekends noon until 11.00pm
Telephone Nº: (0113) 255-7292

GROUND INFORMATION
Away Supporters' Entrances & Sections:
No usual segregation

ADMISSION INFO (2006/2007 PRICES)
Adult Standing: £8.50
Adult Seating: £8.50
Senior Citizen Standing: £4.50
Senior Citizen Seating: £4.50
Child Standing: £4.50
Child Seating: £4.50
Programme Price: £1.50 (price may change)

DISABLED INFORMATION
Wheelchairs: Accommodated
Helpers: Please phone the club for information
Prices: Please phone the club for information
Disabled Toilets: Available
Contact: (0113) 255-7292 (Bookings are necessary)

Travelling Supporters' Information:
Routes: From the North: Take the A1 to Wetherby then the A58 to Leeds. After about 8 miles take the 3rd exit at the roundabout onto the A6120 Ring Road. Follow signs for Bradford for approximately 12 miles and at the 7th roundabout take the B6157 signposted Stanningley. Continue for ½ mile passing the Police Station on the left then turn left down New Street (at the Tradex Warehouse). Turn right into Newlands and the ground is situated at the end of the road next to a new housing development.

GAINSBOROUGH TRINITY FC

Founded: 1873
Former Names: None
Nickname: 'The Blues'
Ground: Northolme, Gainsborough, Lincolnshire, DN21 2QW
Record Attendance: 9,760 (1948)
Pitch Size: 111 × 71 yards

Colours: Blue shirts with White shorts
Telephone Nº: (01427) 613295 or 614134
Clubhouse Phone Nº: (01427) 613688
Fax Number: (01427) 613295
Ground Capacity: 4,340
Seating Capacity: 504
Web site: www.gainsboroughtrinity.com

GENERAL INFORMATION

Supporters Club: G. Burton, c/o Club
Telephone Nº: (01427) 613688
Car Parking: Street parking, in a Local Car Tyre Company car park and also in a Local Authority Car Park nearby
Coach Parking: Opposite the ground
Nearest Railway Station: Lea Road (2 miles)
Nearest Bus Station: Heaton Street (1 mile)
Club Shop: At the ground
Opening Times: Matchdays only
Telephone Nº: (01427) 611612
Police Telephone Nº: (01427) 810910

GROUND INFORMATION

Away Supporters' Entrances & Sections:
No usual segregation

ADMISSION INFO (2006/2007 PRICES)

Adult Standing: £8.00
Adult Seating: £9.00
Concessionary Standing: £6.00
Concessionary Seating: £7.00
Under-12s Standing/Seating: £1.00
Children Ages 12 to 16 Standing/Seating: £2.00
Programme Price: £1.75

DISABLED INFORMATION

Wheelchairs: Accommodated
Helpers: Please phone the club for information
Prices: Normal prices for the disabled. Free for helpers
Disabled Toilets: Available in new block adjacent to the Main Stand
Contact: (01427) 613295 (Bookings are not necessary)

Travelling Supporters' Information:
Routes: From the North, South and West: Exit the A1 at Blyth services taking the 1st left through to Bawtry. In Bawtry, turn right at the traffic lights onto the A631 straight through to Gainsborough (approx. 11 miles). Go over the bridge to the second set of traffic lights and turn left onto the A159 (Scunthorpe Road). Follow the main road past Tesco on the right through the traffic lights. The ground is 250 yards on right opposite the Total Petrol station; From the East: Take the A631 into Gainsborough and turn right onto the A159. Then as above.

HARROGATE TOWN FC

Founded: 1919
Former Names: Harrogate FC and Harrogate Hotspurs FC
Nickname: 'Town'
Ground: Wetherby Road, Harrogate   HG2 7SA
Record Attendance: 4,280 (1950)
Pitch Size: 107 × 72 yards

Colours: Yellow and Black striped shirts, Black shorts
Telephone N°: (01423) 880675 or 883671
Contact N°: (01423) 525341 (Club Secretary)
Contact Fax Number: (01423) 525341
Club Fax Number: (01423) 880675
Ground Capacity: 3,290
Seating Capacity: 502
Web site: www.harrogatetown.com

GENERAL INFORMATION

Supporters Club: c/o Phil Harrison, 14 Chatsworth Grove, Harrogate   HG1 2AS
Telephone/Fax N°: (01423) 525211
Car Parking: Hospital Car Park adjacent
Coach Parking: At the ground
Nearest Railway Station: Harrogate (¾ mile)
Nearest Bus Station: Harrogate
Club Shop: At the ground
Opening Times: Matchdays only
Telephone N°: (01423) 325111
Police Telephone N°: (01423) 505541

GROUND INFORMATION

Away Supporters' Entrances & Sections:
No usual segregation

ADMISSION INFO (2006/2007 PRICES)

Adult Standing: £10.00
Adult Seating: £11.00
Concessionary Standing: £5.00
Concessionary Seating: £6.00
Under-12s Standing: £2.00
Under-12s Seating: £3.00
Programme Price: £2.00

DISABLED INFORMATION

Wheelchairs: Accommodated at the front of the Main Stand
Helpers: Admitted
Prices: Free for the disabled when accompanied by a helper. Normal prices for helpers
Disabled Toilets: Available
Contact: (01423) 880675 (Bookings are not necessary)

Travelling Supporters' Information:
Routes: From the South: Take the A61 from Leeds and turn right at the roundabout onto the ring road (signposted York). After about 1¼ miles turn left at the next roundabout onto A661 Wetherby Road. The ground is situated ¾ mile on the right; From the West: Take the A59 straight into Wetherby Road from Empress Roundabout and the ground is on the left; From the East & North: Exit the A1(M) at Junction 47, take the A59 to Harrogate then follow the Southern bypass to Wetherby Road for the A661 Roundabout. Turn right towards Harrogate Town Centre and the ground is on the right after ¾ mile.

HINCKLEY UNITED FC

Founded: 1889
Former Names: Formed when Hinckley Athletic FC merged with Hinckley Town FC in 1997 (previously Westfield Rovers FC)
Nickname: 'The Knitters'
Ground: Marstons Stadium, Leicester Road, Hinckley, LE10 3DR
Record Attendance: 2,278 (10th December 2005)

Pitch Size: 110 × 72 yards
Colours: Shirts are Blue with Red trim, Blue shorts
Telephone Nº: (01455) 840088
Contact Number: (01455) 840088
Ground Capacity: 4,329
Seating Capacity: 630
Web site: www.hinckleyunitedfc.co.uk

GENERAL INFORMATION
Supporters Club: c/o Club
Telephone Nº: (01455) 840088
Car Parking: At the ground
Coach Parking: At the ground
Nearest Railway Station: Hinckley (2 miles)
Nearest Bus Station: Hinckley
Club Shop: At the ground
Opening Times: Matchdays only
Telephone Nº: (01455) 840088
Police Telephone Nº: (0116) 222-2222

GROUND INFORMATION
Away Supporters' Entrances & Sections:
West Stand and Terrace if required (no usual segregation)

ADMISSION INFO (2006/2007 PRICES)
Adult Standing: £9.00
Adult Seating: £10.00
Under-16s Standing: £3.00
Under-16s Seating: £4.00
Senior Citizen Standing: £6.00
Senior Citizen Seating: £7.00
Programme Price: £2.00

DISABLED INFORMATION
Wheelchairs: Accommodated
Helpers: Admitted
Prices: Normal prices apply
Disabled Toilets: Yes
Contact: (01455) 840088   (Bookings are not necessary)

Travelling Supporters' Information:
Routes: From the North-West: Take the A5 southbound and take the 1st exit at Dodwells roundabout onto the A47 towards Earl Shilton. Go straight on over 3 roundabouts then take the 3rd exit at the next roundabout onto the B4668. The entrance to the ground is on the right after 200 yards; From the South: Take the A5 northbound and upon reaching Dodwells roundabout take the 2nd exit onto the A47 towards East Shilton. Then as above; From the North-East: Take the M69, exit at Junction 2 and follow the B4669 towards Hinckley. After 2 miles (passing through 2 sets of traffic lights) bear right into Spa Lane then turn right at the next set of traffic lights onto the B4668 towards Earl Shilton. The Stadium is on the left after 1¾ miles.

HUCKNALL TOWN FC

Founded: 1946
Former Names: Hucknall Colliery Welfare FC
Nickname: 'The Town'
Ground: Watnall Road, Hucknall, Nottinghamshire, NG15 6EY
Record Attendance: 1,836 (9th April 2005)
Pitch Size: 111 × 72 yards

Colours: Yellow shirts with Black shorts
Social Club Telephone Nº: (0115) 956-1253
Daytime Nº: (0115) 963-0206 (10.00am–4.00pm)
Fax Number: (0115) 963-0716
Ground Capacity: 3,000
Seating Capacity: 500
Web site: www.hucknalltownfc.com

GENERAL INFORMATION

Supporters Club: Mike Drury
Telephone Nº: (0115) 963-0206
Car Parking: Available at the ground
Coach Parking: At the ground
Nearest Railway Station: Hucknall (1 mile)
Nearest Bus Station: Broadmarsh, Nottingham (change for Hucknall)
Club Shop: At the ground
Opening Times: Matchdays or by appointment only
Telephone Nº: (0115) 963-0206
Police Telephone Nº: (0115) 968-0999

GROUND INFORMATION

Away Supporters' Entrances & Sections:
No usual segregation

ADMISSION INFO (2006/2007 PRICES)

Adult Standing: £9.00
Adult Seating: £9.00
Child Standing: £2.00   (Junior Members £1.00)
Child Seating: £2.00   (Junior Members £1.00)
Senior Citizen Standing: £6.00
Senior Citizen Seating: £6.00
Programme Price: £2.00

DISABLED INFORMATION

Wheelchairs: Accommodated
Helpers: Admitted
Prices: Concessionary prices are charged
Disabled Toilets: One available
Contact: (0115) 963-0206 (Bookings are not necessary)

Travelling Supporters' Information:
Routes: Exit the M1 at Junction 27 and take the A608 towards Hucknall. Turn right onto the A611 to Hucknall then take the Hucknall bypass. At the second roundabout join Watnall Road (B6009) and the ground is 100 yards on the right.

HYDE UNITED FC

Founded: 1919
Former Names: Hyde FC (1885-1917)
Nickname: 'Tigers'
Ground: Tameside Stadium, Ewen Fields, Walker Lane, Hyde, Cheshire SK14 2SB
Record Attendance: 9,500 (1952)
Pitch Size: 114 × 70 yards
Colours: Red shirts with White shorts

Telephone Nº: (0161) 368-1031 (Matchdays)
Daytime Phone Nº: (0161) 368-1031 or (07778) 792502 (Secretary)
Fax Number: (0161) 367-7273 (Ground); (01270) 212473 (Secretary)
Ground Capacity: 4,250
Seating Capacity: 550
Web site: www.hydeunited.co.uk

GENERAL INFORMATION
Supporters Club: Mark Dring, 16 Gainsborough Walk, Denton, Manchester M34 6NS
Telephone Nº: (0161) 336-8076
Car Parking: 150 spaces available at the ground
Coach Parking: At the ground
Nearest Railway Station: Newton (¼ mile)
Nearest Bus Station: Hyde
Club Shop: At the ground
Opening Times: Matchdays only
Telephone Nº: (0161) 368-1031
Police Telephone Nº: (0161) 330-8321

GROUND INFORMATION
Away Supporters' Entrances & Sections:
No usual segregation although it is used as required

ADMISSION INFO (2006/2007 PRICES)
Adult Standing: £9.00
Adult Seating: £10.00
Child Standing: £3.00
Child Seating: £4.00
Senior Citizen Standing: £3.00
Senior Citizen Seating: £4.00
Programme Price: £1.50

DISABLED INFORMATION
Wheelchairs: Accommodated in the disabled area
Helpers: Please phone the club for information
Prices: Please phone the club for information
Disabled Toilets: Yes
Contact: (01270) 212473 (Bookings are not necessary)

Travelling Supporters' Information:
Routes: Exit the M60 at Junction 24 and then exit the M67 at Junction 3 for Hyde. Turn right at the top of the slip road, left at the lights (Morrisons on the left). Turn right at the next set of lights into Lumn Road then turn left at the Give Way sign into Walker Lane. Take the 2nd Car Park entrance near the Leisure Pool and follow the road round for the Stadium.

KETTERING TOWN FC

Founded: 1872
Former Names: None
Nickname: 'The Poppies'
Ground: Rockingham Road, Kettering, Northants. NN16 9AW
Record Attendance: 11,526 (1947-48)
Pitch Size: 110 × 70 yards

Colours: Red shirts and shorts
Telephone Nº: (01536) 483028/410815
Daytime Phone Nº: (01536) 483028
Fax Number: (01536) 412273
Ground Capacity: 6,264
Seating Capacity: 1,747
Web site: www.ketteringtownfc.co.uk
E-mail: info@ketteringtownfc.co.uk

GENERAL INFORMATION

Supporters Club: c/o Club
Car Parking: At the ground
Coach Parking: At the 'Beeswing' Public House
Nearest Railway Station: Kettering (1 mile)
Nearest Bus Station: Kettering (1 mile)
Club Shop: At the ground. Also at Elmore's News Shop in Silver Street, Kettering
Opening Times: Shop hours in the Town Centre shop and on request at the ground on Matchdays
Telephone Nº: (01536) 483028
Police Telephone Nº: (01536) 411411

GROUND INFORMATION

Away Supporters' Entrances & Sections:
Rockingham Road End accommodation

ADMISSION INFO (2006/2007 PRICES)

Adult Standing: £10.00
Adult Seating: £12.00
Senior Citizen Standing: £8.50
Senior Citizen Seating: £10.50
Note: Children up to the age of 16 years may apply for a £45.00 season ticket.
Programme Price: £2.50

DISABLED INFORMATION

Wheelchairs: 12 spaces are available on the terracing adjacent to the Main Stand
Helpers: One helper admitted per wheelchair
Prices: Free of charge for the disabled
Disabled Toilets: Available next to the Social Club
Contact: (01536) 483028 (Bookings are not necessary)

Travelling Supporters' Information:
Routes: To reach Kettering from the A1, M1 or M6, use the A14 to Junction 7, follow the A43 for 1 mile, turn right at the roundabout and the ground is 400 yards on the left on the A6003. (The ground is situated to the North of Kettering (1 mile) on the main A6003 Rockingham Road to Oakham).

LANCASTER CITY FC

Founded: 1905
Former Names: Lancaster Athletic FC,
Lancaster Town FC and City of Lancaster AFC
Nickname: 'Dolly Blues'
Ground: Giant Axe, West Road, Lancaster LA1 5PE
Record Attendance: 7,500 (1936)
Pitch Size: 110 × 70 yards

Colours: Sky Blue shirts and shorts
Telephone Nº: (01524) 382238/841710 (Office)
Ground Phone Nº: (01524) 382238
Fax Number: (01524) 382238
Ground Capacity: 3,153
Seating Capacity: 513
Web site: www.lancastercityfc.com

GENERAL INFORMATION

Supporters Club: At the Dolly Blue Tavern
Telephone Nº: (01524) 843500
Car Parking: At the ground
Coach Parking: At the ground
Nearest Railway Station: Lancaster (2 minutes walk)
Nearest Bus Station: Lancaster (5 minutes walk)
Club Shop: At the ground
Opening Times: Matchdays only
Telephone Nº: None
Police Telephone Nº: (01524) 63333

GROUND INFORMATION

Away Supporters' Entrances & Sections:
No usual segregation

ADMISSION INFO (2006/2007 PRICES)

Adult Standing: £8.00
Adult Seating: £8.00
Concession/Child Standing: £5.00
Concession/Child Seating: £5.00
Children under the age of 4 are admitted free of charge
Programme Price: £1.50

DISABLED INFORMATION

Wheelchairs: Accommodated
Helpers: Admitted
Prices: Normal prices apply
Disabled Toilets: Yes
Contact: (01524) 382238 (Bookings are not necessary)

Travelling Supporters' Information:
Routes: From the South: Exit the M6 at Junction 33 and follow Railway Station signs into the City. Turn left at the traffic lights after Waterstones Bookshop then take the second right passing the Railway Station on the right. Follow the road down the hill and the ground is 1st right; From the North: Exit the M6 at Junction 34 and bear left onto the A683. Go into the one-way system in the City and pass the Police Station. At the next traffic lights by the Alexandra pub, follow the road back into the centre, then as from the South, following Railway Station signs.

LEIGH RMI FC

Founded: 1896
Former Names: Horwich RMI FC
Nickname: 'The Railwaymen'
Ground: Hilton Park, Kirkhall Lane, Leigh, WN7 1RN
Record Attendance: 9,853 (1949)
Pitch Size: 112 × 75 yards

Colours: Red and White shirts with Red shorts
Telephone Nº: (01772) 719266
Fax Number: (01772) 719266
Ground Capacity: 8,500
Seating Capacity: 1,425
Web site: www.leighrmi.com

GENERAL INFORMATION
Supporters Club: c/o Club
Car Parking: 150 spaces available at the ground
Coach Parking: At the ground
Nearest Railway Station: Atherton
Nearest Bus Station: Leigh
Club Shop: At the ground
Opening Times: Daily
Telephone Nº: (01942) 743743
Police Telephone Nº: (01942) 244981

GROUND INFORMATION
Away Supporters' Entrances & Sections:
No usual segregation

ADMISSION INFO (2006/2007 PRICES)
Adult Standing: £10.00
Adult Seating: £10.00
Child/Senior Citizen Standing: £5.00
Child/Senior Citizen Seating: £5.00
Junior Members Standing/Seating: £1.00
Programme Price: £1.50

DISABLED INFORMATION
Wheelchairs: Accommodated by arrangement
Helpers: Admitted
Prices: Normal prices apply
Disabled Toilets: Four available at the ground
Contact: (01772) 719266   (Bookings are not necessary)

Travelling Supporters' Information:
Routes: Exit the M61 at Junction 5 and follow the Westhoughton sign to the roundabout then follow signs for Leigh. Stay on the main road to the traffic lights, turn left into Leigh Road and carry on for about 3 miles until the traffic lights. Turn left and then 1st right at the next set of traffic lights. Turn right onto Atheleigh Way (A579) at the first set of traffic lights and turn left (B & Q on the right), at the next set of traffic lights. Turn right (Leigh Town Centre), at the second opening on the right turn into Prescott Street, carry on to the top, turn right and the ground is on the left.

MOOR GREEN FC

Moor Green FC are groundsharing with Solihull Borough for the 2006/2007 Season

Founded: 1901
Former Names: None
Nickname: 'The Moors'
Ground: Damson Park, Damson Parkway, Solihull, B91 2PP
Ground Record Attendance: 2,000
Pitch Size: 110 × 75 yards

Colours: Shirts are Sky & Dark Blue halves, shorts are Dark Blue
Contact Telephone Nº: (0121) 476-4944 or 07801 248211
Correspondence: N.Collins, 7 The Morelands, West Heath, Birmingham   B31 3HA
Ground Capacity: 3,050   **Seating Capacity**: 280
Web site: www.moorgreenfc.co.uk

GENERAL INFORMATION
Supporters Club: –
Car Parking: At the ground
Coach Parking: At the ground
Nearest Railway Station: Birmingham International (2 miles)
Nearest Bus Station: Birmingham (5 miles)
Club Shop: None
Opening Times: –
Telephone Nº: –
Police Telephone Nº: (0121) 706-8111

GROUND INFORMATION
Away Supporters' Entrances & Sections:
No usual segregation

ADMISSION INFO (2006/2007 PRICES)
Adult Standing: £9.00
Adult Seating: £9.00
Senior Citizen/Junior Standing: £4.00
Senior Citizen/Junior Seating: £4.00
Programme Price: £1.50

DISABLED INFORMATION
Wheelchairs: Spaces for 3 wheelchairs are available
Helpers: Admitted
Prices: Normal prices apply
Disabled Toilets: Available
Contact: (0121) 705-6770 (Matchdays only)

Travelling Supporters' Information:
Routes: Exit the M42 at Junction 6 and take the A45 for 2 miles towards Birmingham. Turn left at the traffic lights near the Posthouse Hotel into Damson Parkway (signposted for Landrover/Damsonwood). Continue to the roundabout and come back along the other carriageway to the ground which is situated on the left after about 150 yards.

NUNEATON BOROUGH FC

The club expect to move to a new stadium in Liberty Way in 2007.
Please contact the club directly for further information.

Founded: 1937 (Reformed 1991)
Former Names: Nuneaton Town FC
Nickname: 'Boro'
Ground: Manor Park, Beaumont Road, Nuneaton, Warwickshire CV11 5HD
Record Attendance: 22,114 (1967)
Pitch Size: 112 × 77 yards

Colours: Blue shirts and white shorts
Telephone N°: (024) 7638-5738
Daytime Phone N°: (024) 7638-5738
Fax Number: (024) 7634-2690
Ground Capacity: 6,000
Seating Capacity: 550
Web site: www.nbafc.net

GENERAL INFORMATION
Supporters Club: c/o Manor Park
Car Parking: Street parking only
Coach Parking: At the ground
Nearest Railway Station: Nuneaton (2 miles)
Nearest Bus Station: Nuneaton (2 miles)
Club Shop: Yes – The Boro Shop
Opening Times: Daily from 10.00am to 4.00pm
Telephone N°: (024) 7638-5738
Police Telephone N°: (024) 7664-1111

GROUND INFORMATION
Away Supporters' Entrances & Sections:
Top Cock and Bear entrances for Canal Side accommodation when segregated

ADMISSION INFO (2006/2007 PRICES)
Adult Standing: £8.00
Adult Seating: £10.00
Concessionary Standing: £5.00
Concessionary Seating: £7.00
Programme Price: £2.00

DISABLED INFORMATION
Wheelchairs: Accommodated
Helpers: Please phone the club for information
Prices: Please phone the club for information
Disabled Toilets: Available at rear of Main Stand
Contact: (024) 7638-5738 (Bookings are not necessary)

Travelling Supporters' Information:
Routes: Exit the M6 at Junction 3 and take the A444 to Nuneaton. At the roundabout by the hospital immediately after the pedestrian overbridge, turn left into College Street to the Bull Ring. Turn right into Greenmoor Road and follow ¾ mile to the end, then turn right and cross over the bridge – the ground is on the left.

REDDITCH UNITED FC

Founded: 1891	**Colours**: Red shirts, shorts and socks
Former Names: Redditch Town FC	**Telephone Nº**: (01527) 67450
Nickname: 'The Reds'	**Contact Nº**: (01527) 67450
Ground: Valley Stadium, Bromsgrove Road, Redditch B97 4RN	**Fax Number**: (01527) 67450
	Ground Capacity: 5,000
Record Attendance: 5,500 (vs Bromsgrove 1954/55)	**Seating Capacity**: 400
Pitch Size: 110 × 72 yards	**Web site**: www.redditchunited.com

GENERAL INFORMATION

Supporters Club: c/o Club
Telephone Nº: (01527) 67450
Car Parking: At the ground
Coach Parking: At the ground
Nearest Railway Station: Redditch (¼ mile)
Nearest Bus Station: Redditch (¼ mile)
Club Shop: None

GROUND INFORMATION

Away Supporters' Entrances & Sections:
No segregation

ADMISSION INFO (2006/2007 PRICES)

Adult Standing: £7.00
Adult Seating: £8.00
Senior Citizen Standing: £5.00
Senior Citizen Seating: £6.00
Under-12s: £2.00 when accompanied by a paying adult
Programme Price: £1.60

DISABLED INFORMATION

Wheelchairs: Accommodated
Helpers: Admitted
Prices: Normal prices apply to both helpers and disabled
Disabled Toilets: Available
Contact: (01527) 67450   (Bookings are not necessary)

Travelling Supporters' Information:
Routes: Exit the M42 at Junction 2 and follow the A441 towards Redditch. Take the 4th exit at the roundabout (signposted Batchley) and turn left at the traffic lights into Birmingham Road. Take the next right into Clive Road then left into Hewell Road. Continue to the T-junction and turn right, passing the Railway Station on the right. Continue through the traffic lights and the ground is situated on the right hand side after about ¼ mile.

SCARBOROUGH FC

Founded: 1879
Former Names: None
Nickname: 'Boro' 'Seadogs'
Ground: McCain Stadium, Seamer Road, Scarborough, North Yorkshire   YO12 4HF
Record Attendance: 11,124 (1938)
Pitch Size: 112 × 74 yards

Colours: Red shirts and shorts
Telephone Nº: (01723) 375094
Fax Number: (01723) 366211
Ground Capacity: 6,161
Seating Capacity: 2,963
Web site: www.scarboroughfc.com

GENERAL INFORMATION
Supporters Club: Stuart Canvin. 97 Seamer Road, Scarborough
Telephone Nº: (07736) 228315
Car Parking: Street parking
Coach Parking: As directed by the Stewards
Nearest Railway Station: Scarborough Central (2 miles)
Nearest Bus Station: Town Centre (2 miles)
Club Shop: At the ground
Opening Times: Weekdays & Matchdays 9.00am – 1.00pm
Telephone Nº: (01723) 375094
Police Telephone Nº: (01723) 500300

GROUND INFORMATION
Away Supporters' Entrances & Sections:
West Stand turnstiles for West Stand seating only (enter from Edgehill Road)

ADMISSION INFO (2006/2007 PRICES)
Adult Admission: £12.00
Child Admission (Under-16s): £5.00
Senior Citizen Admission: £8.00
Note: Prices include seating at both ends of the ground. An extra £2.00 fee is charged for admission to the Grandstand
Programme Price: £2.50

DISABLED INFORMATION
Wheelchairs: 20 spaces in total in the Main Stand, West Stand and East Stand
Helpers: One helper admitted per wheelchair
Prices: Normal prices for the wheelchair disabled. Free of charge for helpers
Disabled Toilets: Available at rear of disabled area
Contact: (01723) 375094   (Bookings are not necessary)

Travelling Supporters' Information:
Routes: The ground is situated on the main York to Scarborough Road (A64), ½ mile on the left past the B&Q DIY store.

STALYBRIDGE CELTIC FC

Founded: 1909
Former Names: None
Nickname: 'Celtic'
Ground: Bower Fold, Mottram Road, Stalybridge, Cheshire SK15 2RT
Record Attendance: 9,753 (1922/23)
Pitch Size: 109 × 70 yards

Colours: Blue shirts and shorts
Telephone N°: (0161) 338-2828
Daytime Phone N°: (0161) 338-2828
Fax Number: (0161) 338-8256
Ground Capacity: 6,108
Seating Capacity: 1,155
Web site: www.stalybridgeceltic.co.uk

GENERAL INFORMATION

Supporters Club: Bob Rhodes, c/o Club
Telephone N°: (01457) 764044
Car Parking: At the ground
Coach Parking: At the ground
Nearest Railway Station: Stalybridge (1 mile)
Nearest Bus Station: Stalybridge town centre
Club Shop: At the ground
Opening Times: Matchdays and by arrangement
Telephone N°: (0161) 338-2828
Police Telephone N°: (0161) 330-8321

GROUND INFORMATION

Away Supporters' Entrances & Sections:
Lockwood & Greenwood Stand

ADMISSION INFO (2006/2007 PRICES)

Adult Standing: £10.00
Adult Seating: £10.00
Under-14s Standing/Seating: Free of charge
Concessionary Standing: £6.00
Concessionary Seating: £6.00
Programme Price: £2.00

DISABLED INFORMATION

Wheelchairs: 20 spaces available each for home and away fans at the side of the Stepan Stand. A further 9 spaces available in the new Lord Tom Pendry Stand
Helpers: Please phone the club for information
Prices: Please phone the club for information
Disabled Toilets: Available at the rear of the Stepan Stand and at the side of the Lord Tom Pendry Stand
Contact: (0161) 338-2828   (Bookings are necessary)

Travelling Supporters' Information:
Routes: From the Midlands and South: Take the M6, M56, M60 and M67, leaving at the end of the motorway. Go across the roundabout to the traffic lights and turn left. The ground is approximately 2 miles on the left before the Hare & Hounds pub; From the North: Exit the M62 at Junction 18 onto the M60 singposted for Ashton-under-Lyne. Follow the M60 to Junction 24 and join the M67, then as from the Midlands and South.

VAUXHALL MOTORS FC

Founded: 1963
Former Names: Vauxhall GM FC
Nickname: 'Motormen'
Ground: Rivacre Park, Hooton, Ellesmere Port, Cheshire   CH66 1NJ
Record Attendance: 1,500 (1987)
Pitch Size: 110 × 70 yards
Colours: White shirts with Dark Blue shorts

Telephone Nº: (0151) 328-1114 (Ground)
Ground Capacity: 2,500
Seating Capacity: 350
Contact: Carole Paisey, 31 South Road, West Kirby, Wirral CH48 3HG
Contact Phone and Fax Nº: (0151) 625-6936
Web site: www.vmfc.com
E-mail: office@vmfc.com

GENERAL INFORMATION
Supporters Club: At the ground
Telephone/Fax Nº: (0151) 328-1114
Car Parking: At the ground
Coach Parking: At the ground
Nearest Railway Station: Hooton
Nearest Bus Station: Ellesmere Port
Club Shop: At the ground
Opening Times: Matchdays only
Telephone Nº: –

GROUND INFORMATION
Away Supporters' Entrances & Sections:
No usual segregation

ADMISSION INFO (2006/2007 PRICES)
Adult Standing/Seating: £8.00
Child Standing/Seating: £3.00
Senior Citizen Standing/Seating: £5.00
Programme Price: £2.00

DISABLED INFORMATION
Wheelchairs: Accommodated as necessary
Helpers: Admitted
Prices: Normal prices for the disabled. Free for helpers
Disabled Toilets: Available
Contact: – (Bookings are not necessary)

Travelling Supporters' Information:
Routes: Exit the M53 at Junction 5 and take the A41 towards Chester. Turn left at the first set of traffic lights into Hooton Green. Turn left at the first T-junction then right at the next T-junction into Rivacre Road. The ground is situated 250 yards on the right.

WORCESTER CITY FC

Founded: 1902
Former Names: Berwick Rangers FC
Nickname: 'The City'
Ground: St. Georges Lane, Worcester   WR1 1QT
Record Attendance: 17,042 (1958/59)
Pitch Size: 110 × 75 yards

Colours: Blue and White shirts with Blue shorts
Telephone Nº: (01905) 23003
Fax Number: (01905) 26668
Ground Capacity: 4,500
Seating Capacity: 1,100
Web site: www.worcestercityfc.co.uk

GENERAL INFORMATION

Supporters Club: P. Gardner, c/o Club
Telephone Nº: –
Car Parking: Street parking
Coach Parking: Street parking
Nearest Railway Station: Foregate Street (1 mile)
Nearest Bus Station: Crowngate Bus Station
Club Shop: At the ground
Opening Times: Matchdays only 10.00am – 5.00pm
Telephone Nº: (01905) 23003
Police Telephone Nº: (01905) 723888

GROUND INFORMATION

Away Supporters' Entrances & Sections:
Turnstile at the Canal End when segregation in in force for Canal End accommodation

ADMISSION INFO (2006/2007 PRICES)

Adult Standing: £10.00
Adult Seating: £11.00
Child/Senior Citizen Standing: £5.00
Child/Senior Citizen Seating: £6.00
Programme Price: £2.00

DISABLED INFORMATION

Wheelchairs: 3 covered spaces available
Helpers: Please phone the club for information
Prices: Please phone the club for information
Disabled Toilets: None
Contact: (01905) 23003   (Bookings are necessary)

Travelling Supporters' Information:
Routes: Exit the M5 at Junction 6 and take the A449 Kidderminster Road. Follow to the end of the dual carriageway and take the second exit at the roundabout for Worcester City Centre. At the first set of traffic lights turn right into the town centre. The 3rd turning on the left is St. Georges Lane.

WORKINGTON AFC

Founded: 1884 (Reformed 1921)
Former Names: None
Nickname: 'Reds'
Ground: Borough Park, Workington   CA14 2DT
Record Attendance: 21,000 (vs Manchester United)
Pitch Size: 110 × 71 yards

Colours: Red shirts and shorts
Telephone Nº: (01900) 602871
Fax Number: (01900) 67432
Ground Capacity: 3,100
Seating Capacity: 500
Web site: www.workingtonafc.co.uk

GENERAL INFORMATION
Supporters Club: Yes
Car Parking: Car Park next to the ground
Coach Parking: At the ground
Nearest Railway Station: Workington (¼ mile)
Nearest Bus Station: Workington (½ mile)
Club Shop: At the ground
Opening Times: Matchdays only
Telephone Nº: (01946) 832710

GROUND INFORMATION
Away Supporters' Entrances & Sections:
No usual segregation

ADMISSION INFO (2006/2007 PRICES)
Adult Standing: £8.00
Adult Seating: £8.00
Senior Citizen/Junior Standing: £4.00
Senior Citizen/Junior Seating: £4.00
Programme Price: £1.50

DISABLED INFORMATION
Wheelchairs: Accommodated
Helpers: Admitted
Prices: Normal prices apply
Disabled Toilets: Available
Contact: (01900) 602871   (Bookings are not necessary)

Travelling Supporters' Information:
Routes: Exit the M6 at Junction 40 and take the A66 towards Keswick and Workington. Upon reaching Workington, continue until you reach the traffic lights at a T-junction. Turn right here onto the A596 for Maryport. After approximately ½ mile you will see the ground floodlights on the opposite site of the river (to the left). Continue along the A596, pass under the bridge taking the next right signposted for the Stadium. The ground is then on the left hand side opposite the Tesco superstore.

WORKSOP TOWN FC

Founded: 1861 (Reformed in 1893)
Former Names: None
Nickname: 'The Tigers'
Ground: Babbage Way, off Sandy Lane, Worksop, Nottinghamshire S80 1TN
Record Attendance: 2,115
Pitch Size: 110 × 72 yards

Colours: Amber shirts with Black shorts
Telephone Nº: (01909) 501911
Fax Number: (01909) 487934
Ground Capacity: 2,500
Seating Capacity: 1,000
Web site: www.worksoptownfc.co.uk

GENERAL INFORMATION
Supporters Club: c/o Club
Telephone Nº: (01909) 501911
Car Parking: Adjacent to the ground
Coach Parking: Adjacent to the ground
Nearest Railway Station: Worksop (2 minutes walk)
Nearest Bus Station: Worksop (2 minutes walk)
Club Shop: At the ground
Opening Times: Matchdays only
Telephone Nº: (01909) 501911
Police Telephone Nº: (01909) 470999

GROUND INFORMATION
Away Supporters' Entrances & Sections:
No usual segregation

ADMISSION INFO (2006/2007 PRICES)
Adult Standing: £9.00
Adult Seating: £9.00
Child Standing: £4.00
Child Seating: £4.00
Programme Price: £2.00

DISABLED INFORMATION
Wheelchairs: Accommodated
Helpers: Admitted
Prices: £3.00 for the disabled. Helpers charged normal prices
Disabled Toilets: Yes
Contact: (01909) 501911 (Bookings are not necessary)

Travelling Supporters' Information:
Routes: Exit the M1 at Junction 31 from the North or at Junction 30 from the South and follow signs for Worksop. After reaching Worksop carry on to the bypass and at the 3rd roundabout (next to Sainsburys) turn off following signs for Sandy Lane Industrial Estate. The ground is ½ mile on the left.

THE NATIONWIDE FOOTBALL CONFERENCE SOUTH CLUBS

Address

Riverside House, 14B High Street,
Crayford, Kent   DA1 4HG

Phone (01322) 411021   **Fax** (01322) 411022

Clubs for the 2006/2007 Season

BASINGSTOKE TOWN FC

Founded: 1896
Former Names: None
Nickname: 'Dragons'
Ground: The Camrose Ground, Western Way,
Basingstoke, Hants.   RG22 6EZ
Record Attendance: 5,085 (25/11/97)
Pitch Size: 110 × 70 yards

Colours: Yellow and Blue shirts with Blue shorts
Telephone Nº: (01256) 327575
Fax Number: (01256) 869997
Social Club Nº: (01256) 464353
Ground Capacity: 6,000
Seating Capacity: 650
Web site: www.btfc.co.uk

GENERAL INFORMATION

Supporters Club: c/o Club
Telephone Nº: (01256) 327575
Car Parking: 600 spaces available at the ground
Coach Parking: Ample room available at ground
Nearest Railway Station: Basingstoke
Nearest Bus Station: Basingstoke Town Centre (2 miles)
Club Shop: The Camrose Shop
Opening Times: Matchdays only
Telephone Nº: (01256) 327575
Police Telephone Nº: (01256) 473111

GROUND INFORMATION

Away Supporters' Entrances & Sections:
No usual segregation

ADMISSION INFO (2006/2007 PRICES)

Adult Standing: £9.00
Adult Seating: £10.00
Concessionary Standing: £5.00
Concessionary Seating: £6.00
Under 14's Standing: £2.00
Under 14's Seating: £3.00
Programme Price: £1.50

DISABLED INFORMATION

Wheelchairs: 6 spaces are available under cover
Helpers: Admitted
Prices: Normal prices for the disabled. Free for helpers
Disabled Toilets: Yes
Contact: (01256) 327575   (Bookings are not necessary)

Travelling Supporters' Information:
Routes: Exit the M3 at Junction 6 and take the 1st left at the Black Dam roundabout. At the next roundabout take the 2nd exit, then the 1st exit at the following roundabout and the 5th exit at the next roundabout. This takes you into Western Way and the ground is 50 yards on the right.

BEDFORD TOWN FC

Founded: 1908 (Re-formed in 1989)
Former Names: None
Nickname: 'Eagles'
Ground: The Eyrie, Meadow Lane, Cardington, Bedford MK44 3SB
Record Attendance: 3,000 (6/8/93)
Pitch Size: 110 × 72 yards

Colours: Shirts are Blue with White trim, Blue shorts
Telephone Nº: (01234) 831558
Fax Number: (01234) 831990
Ground Capacity: 3,000
Seating Capacity: 300
Web site: www.bedfordeagles.net
E-mail: david.swallow@bedfordeagles.net

GENERAL INFORMATION
Supporters Club: c/o Club
Car Parking: At the ground
Coach Parking: At the ground
Nearest Railway Station: Bedford Midland (3 miles)
Nearest Bus Station: Greyfriars, Bedford (3 miles)
Club Shop: At the ground
Opening Times: Matchdays only
Telephone Nº: (01234) 831558
Police Telephone Nº: (01234) 271212

GROUND INFORMATION
Away Supporters' Entrances & Sections:
No usual segregation

ADMISSION INFO (2006/2007 PRICES)
Adult Standing: £9.00
Adult Seating: £10.00
Concessionary Standing: £6.00
Concessionary Seating: £7.00
Children Aged 13 and under Standing: £2.00
Children Aged 13 and under Seating: £3.00
Programme Price: £1.50

DISABLED INFORMATION
Wheelchairs: Accommodated
Helpers: Admitted
Prices: Normal prices apply
Disabled Toilets: Available
Contact: (01234) 831558 (Bookings are not necessary)

Travelling Supporters' Information:
Routes: From the M1: Exit the M1 at Junction 13 onto the A421. Follow this the the bypass at the Sandy exit and take the A603 towards Sandy. The ground is on the left just before the lay-by; From the A1: Take the Sandy exit, go through Willington and the ground is on the right; From Bedford: Follow signs for Sandy and take Cardington Road out of town. The ground is on the left past 2 mini-roundabouts.

BISHOP'S STORTFORD FC

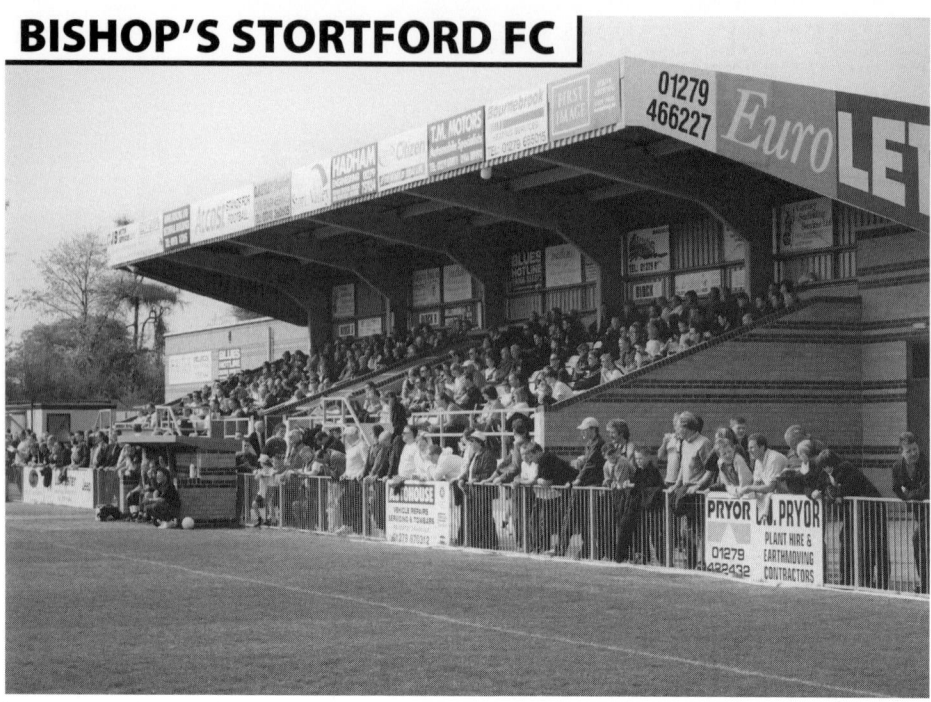

Founded: 1874
Former Names: None
Nickname: 'Blues' 'Bishops'
Ground: Woodside Park, Dunmow Road,
Bishop's Stortford   CM23 5RG
Record Attendance: 3,555 (2000)
Pitch Size: 110 × 70 yards

Colours: Blue and White shirts with Blue shorts
Telephone Nº: (08700) 339930
Fax Number: (08700) 339931
Ground Capacity: 4,000
Seating Capacity: 298
Web site: www.bsfc.co.uk

GENERAL INFORMATION

Supporters Club: None
Car Parking: 150 spaces available at the ground
Coach Parking: At the ground
Nearest Railway Station: Bishop's Stortford
Nearest Bus Station: Bishop's Stortford
Club Shop: At the ground
Opening Times: Matchdays only 1.30pm to 5.00pm
Telephone Nº: (08700) 339930
Police Telephone Nº: –

GROUND INFORMATION

Away Supporters' Entrances & Sections:
No usual segregation

ADMISSION INFO (2006/2007 PRICES)

Adult Standing: £10.00
Adult Seating: £10.00
Child Standing: £6.00
Child Seating: £6.00
Family Tickets: 1 Adult + 2 Children £18.00;
2 Adults + 2 Children £25.00
Programme Price: £2.00

DISABLED INFORMATION

Wheelchairs: Accommodated in the disabled section
Helpers: Admitted
Prices: Free of charge for the disabled and helpers
Disabled Toilets: Yes
Contact: (08700) 339930   (Bookings are not necessary)

Travelling Supporters' Information:
Routes: Exit the M11 at junction 8 and take the A1250 towards Bishop Stortford. Turn left at the first roundabout and the ground is first right opposite the Golf Club (the entrance is between Industrial Units).

BOGNOR REGIS TOWN FC

Founded: 1883
Former Names: None
Nickname: 'The Rocks'
Ground: Nyewood Lane, Bognor Regis   PO21 2TY
Record Attendance: 3,642 (1984)
Pitch Size: 116 × 75 yards

Colours: White shirts with Green trim, Green shorts
Telephone N°: (01243) 822325
Fax Number: (01243) 866151
Ground Capacity: 6,000
Seating Capacity: 243
Web site: www.therocks.co.uk

GENERAL INFORMATION
Supporters Club: David Seabourne, c/o Club
Telephone N°: (01243) 861336
Car Parking: Outside the ground at the Sports Club
Coach Parking: None
Nearest Railway Station: Bognor Regis (1 mile)
Nearest Bus Station: Bognor Regis (1 mile)
Club Shop: At the ground
Opening Times: Matchdays only
Telephone N°: (01243) 862045
Police Telephone N°: (0845) 607-0999

GROUND INFORMATION
Away Supporters' Entrances & Sections:
No usual segregation

ADMISSION INFO (2006/2007 PRICES)
Adult Standing: £9.00
Adult Seating: £10.00
Senior Citizen Standing: £6.00
Senior Citizen Seating: £7.00
Child Standing: £2.00
Child Seating: £3.00
Programme Price: £1.50

DISABLED INFORMATION
Wheelchairs: Accommodated
Helpers: Admitted
Prices: Normal prices apply
Disabled Toilets: Available
Contact: (01243) 822325   (Bookings are not necessary)

Travelling Supporters' Information:
Routes: From the West: Take the M27/A27 to Chichester then the A259 and pass through Bersted towards Bognor Regis. Turn right into Hawthorne Road then left into Nyewood Lane – the ground is on the right; From the East: Take the A27 from Brighton/Worthing and turn left onto the A29 at Fontwell Roundabout past Denmans Garden Centre. Travel along Shripney Road and turn right at the second roundabout towards Bersted on the A259 then left into Hawthorne Road – then as above.

BRAINTREE TOWN FC

Founded: 1898
Former Names: Manor Works FC, Crittall Athletic FC, Braintree & Crittall Athletic FC and Braintree FC
Nickname: 'The Iron'
Ground: Cressing Road Stadium, Clockhouse Way, Braintree, Essex CM7 6RD
Record Attendance: 4,000 (May 1952)
Pitch Size: 110 × 70 yards

Ground Capacity: 3,400
Seating Capacity: 284
Colours: Yellow shirts and socks
Telephone Nº: (01376) 345617
Fax Number: (01376) 330976
Correspondence Address: Tom Woodley, 19A Bailey Bridge Road, Braintree CM7 5TT
Contact Telephone Nº: (01376) 326234
Web site: www.braintreetownfc.org.uk

GENERAL INFORMATION
Supporters Club: c/o Club
Telephone Nº: (01376) 345617
Car Parking: At the ground
Coach Parking: At the ground
Nearest Railway Station: Braintree & Bocking (1 mile)
Nearest Bus Station: Braintree
Club Shop: At the ground
Opening Times: Matchdays only
Telephone Nº: (01376) 345617

GROUND INFORMATION
Away Supporters' Entrances & Sections: No usual segregation

ADMISSION INFO (2006/2007 PRICES)
Adult Standing: £10.00
Adult Seating: £10.00
Child Standing: £5.00
Child Seating: £5.00
Programme Price: £2.00

DISABLED INFORMATION
Wheelchairs: Accommodated
Helpers: Admitted
Prices: Normal prices apply
Disabled Toilets: Available
Contact: – (Bookings are not necessary)

Travelling Supporters' Information:
Routes: Exit the A120 Braintree Bypass at the McDonald's roundabout following signs for East Braintree Industrial Estate. The floodlights at the ground are visible on the left ½ mile into town. Turn left into Clockhouse Way then left again for the ground.

CAMBRIDGE CITY FC

Founded: 1908
Former Names: Cambridge Town FC
Nickname: 'Lilywhites'
Ground: City Ground, Milton Road, Cambridge, CB4 1UY
Record Attendance: 12,058 (1950)
Pitch Size: 110 × 70 yards

Colours: White shirts with Black shorts
Telephone Nº: (01223) 357973
Fax Number: (01223) 351582
Ground Capacity: 3,000
Seating Capacity: 523
Correspondence: Kevin Peters, 9 Villa Court, Cambridge CB4 2TX
Web site: www.cambridgecityfc.com

GENERAL INFORMATION

Supporters Club: Chris Drummond, c/o Club
Telephone Nº: (01223) 357973
Car Parking: 300 spaces available at the ground
Coach Parking: At the ground
Nearest Railway Station: Cambridge (2 miles)
Nearest Bus Station: Cambridge
Club Shop: At the ground
Opening Times: Matchdays only
Telephone Nº: (01223) 357973
Police Telephone Nº: (01223) 358966

GROUND INFORMATION

Away Supporters' Entrances & Sections:
No usual segregation

ADMISSION INFO (2006/2007 PRICES)

Adult Standing: £9.00
Adult Seating: £9.00
Senior Citizen/Under-16s Standing: £4.00
Senior Citizen/Under-16s Seating: £4.00
Under-11s Standing/Seating: £1.00
Family Ticket: 2 adults + 3 children £15.00
Programme Price: £1.50

DISABLED INFORMATION

Wheelchairs: 6 spaces are available under cover on the half-way line
Helpers: Admitted
Prices: Free of charge for the disabled. One helper admitted free with each disabled fan
Disabled Toilets: One available in the Main Stand
Contact: (01223) 357973 (Bookings are not necessary)

Travelling Supporters' Information:
Routes: Exit the M11 at Junction 13 and take the A1303 into the City. At the end of Madingley Road, turn left into Chesterton Lane and then Chesterton Road. Go into the one-way system and turn left into Milton Road (A10) and the ground is on the left behind the Westbrook Centre.

DORCHESTER TOWN FC

Founded: 1880
Former Names: None
Nickname: 'The Magpies'
Ground: The Avenue Stadium, Weymouth Avenue, Dorchester, Dorset   DT1 2RY
Record Attendance: 4,159 (1/1/99)
Pitch Size: 110 × 80 yards

Colours: Black & White quartered shirts, Black shorts
Telephone Nº: (01305) 262451
Daytime Nº: (01305) 262451 or 262527
Fax Number: (01305) 267623
Ground Capacity: 5,009
Seating Capacity: 710
Web Site: www.the-magpies.net

GENERAL INFORMATION
Supporters Club: H.G. Hill, 39 Thatcham Park, Yeovil, Somerset
Telephone Nº: (01935) 426029
Car Parking: 350 spaces available at the ground
Coach Parking: At the ground
Nearest Railway Station: Dorchester South and West (both 1 mile)
Nearest Bus Station: Nearby
Club Shop: At the ground
Opening Times: During 1st team matchdays only
Telephone Nº: (01305) 262451
Police Telephone Nº: (01305) 251212

GROUND INFORMATION
Away Supporters' Entrances & Sections:
Main Stand side when segregated (not usual)

ADMISSION INFO (2006/2007 PRICES)
Adult Standing: £9.00
Adult Seating: £10.00
Senior Citizen/Child Standing: £5.50
Senior Citizen/Child Seating: £6.50
Under-16s: £1.00 when accompanied by a paying adult
Programme Price: £2.00

DISABLED INFORMATION
Wheelchairs: 10 spaces available each for home and away fans at the North West End of the terracing
Helpers: Admitted
Prices: Normal prices apply
Disabled Toilets: 2 available near the disabled area
Contact: (01305) 262451   (Bookings are not necessary)

Travelling Supporters' Information:
Routes: Take the Dorchester Bypass (A35) from all directions. The ground is on the South side of town, adjacent to a roundabout at the intersection with the A354 to Weymouth. Alternatively, take Weymouth signs from Dorchester Town Centre for 1½ miles.

EASTBOURNE BOROUGH FC

Founded: 1963
Former Names: Langney Sports FC
Nickname: 'The Sports'
Ground: Priory Lane Stadium, Langney Sports Club, Priory Lane, Eastbourne BN23 7QH
Record Attendance: 3,770 (5th November 2005)
Pitch Size: 115 × 72 yards

Colours: Red shirts with Black shorts
Telephone Nº: (01323) 743561
Fax Number: (01323) 741627
Ground Capacity: 5,644
Seating Capacity: 542
Web site: www.eastbourneboroughfc.co.uk

GENERAL INFORMATION

Supporters Club: Yes – c/o Club
Telephone Nº: –
Car Parking: Around 400 spaces available at the ground
Coach Parking: At the ground
Nearest Railway Station: Pevensey & Westham (1½ miles but no public transport to the ground)
Nearest Bus Station: Eastbourne
Club Shop: At the ground
Opening Times: Matchdays only
Telephone Nº: (01323) 743561
Police Telephone Nº: (0845) 607-0999

GROUND INFORMATION

Away Supporters' Entrances & Sections:
No usual segregation

ADMISSION INFO (2006/2007 PRICES)

Adult Standing: £9.50
Adult Seating: £9.50
Child Standing: £2.50 (Under-16s)
Child Seating: £2.50 (Under-16s)
Senior Citizen Standing: £5.50
Senior Citizen Seating: £5.50
Programme Price: £2.00

DISABLED INFORMATION

Wheelchairs: 6 spaces available
Helpers: Admitted
Prices: Normal prices apply
Disabled Toilets: Available
Contact: (01323) 743561 (Bookings are not necessary)

Travelling Supporters' Information:
Routes: Approaching from the A22: Take the first exit to join the Polegate bypass, signposted A27 Eastbourne, Hastings & Bexhill. *Take the 2nd exit at the next roundabout for Stone Cross and Westham (A22) then the first exit at the following roundabout signposted Stone Cross and Westham. Turn right after ½ mile into Friday Street (B2104). At the end of Friday Street, turn left at the double mini-roundabout into Hide Hollow (B2191), passing Eastbourne Crematorium on your right. Turn right at the roundabout into Priory Road, and Priory Lane is about 200 yards down the road on the left; Approaching from the A27 from Brighton: Turn left at the Polegate traffic lights then take 2nd exit at the large roundabout to join the bypass. Then as from *.

FISHER ATHLETIC (LONDON) FC

The club are currently groundsharing with Dulwich Hamlet FC.

Founded: 1908
Former Names: Fisher Athletic FC, Fisher '93 FC
Nickname: 'The Fish'
Ground: Champion Hill Stadium, Edgar Kail Way, London SE22 8BD
Record Attendance: 4,283 (vs Barnet 4/5/1991)
Pitch Size: 110 × 70 yards

Colours: Black and White striped shirts, White shorts
Telephone Nº: (020) 7326-1360
Fax Number: (020) 7326-0163
Ground Capacity: 3,000
Seating Capacity: 500
Web site: www.fisherathletic.co.uk

GENERAL INFORMATION
Supporters Club: None
Telephone Nº: –
Car Parking: 50 spaces available at the ground
Coach Parking: At the ground
Nearest Railway Station: East Dulwich (adjacent)
Nearest Bus Station: East Dulwich
Club Shop: At the ground
Opening Times: Matchdays only
Telephone Nº: (020) 7231-5144
Police Telephone Nº: (020) 8693-3366

GROUND INFORMATION
Away Supporters' Entrances & Sections:
No usual segregation

ADMISSION INFO (2006/2007 PRICES)
Adult Standing: £9.00
Adult Seating: £9.00
Concessionary Standing: £5.00
Concessionary Seating: £5.00
Child Standing: £2.00
Child Seating: £2.00
Programme Price: £1.50

DISABLED INFORMATION
Wheelchairs: Accommodated
Helpers: Please phone the club for information
Prices: Please phone the club for information
Disabled Toilets: Available
Contact: (020) 7231-5144 (Bookings are not necessary)

Travelling Supporters' Information:
Routes: From the Elephant & Castle: Go down Walworth Road, through Camberwell's one-way system and along Denmark Hill. Turn left by the railway into Champion Park and then right at the end down Grave Lane to the ground in Dog Kennel Hill; From the South: Come up through Streatham on the A23, turn right to Tulse Hill along the A205 (Christchurch Road) and carry on towards Sydenham. Turn left at The Grove into Lordship Lane and carry on to East Dulwich.

HAVANT & WATERLOOVILLE FC

Founded: 1998
Former Names: Formed by the amalgamation of Waterlooville FC and Havant Town FC
Nickname: 'The Hawks'
Ground: West Leigh Park, Martin Road, Havant, PO9 5TH
Record Attendance: 3,500 (1985/86)
Pitch Size: 112 × 76 yards

Colours: White shirts and shorts
Telephone Nº: (023) 9278-7822 (Ground)
Fax Number: (023) 9226-2367
Ground Capacity: 5,250
Seating Capacity: 562
Correspondence: Trevor Brock, 2 Betula Close, Waterlooville, PO7 8EJ   **Phone**: (023) 9226-7276
Web site: www.havantandwaterlooville.net

GENERAL INFORMATION

Supporters Club: None, but large Social Club
Telephone Nº: (023) 9278-7855
Car Parking: Space for 750 cars at the ground
Coach Parking: At the ground
Nearest Railway Station: Havant (1 mile)
Nearest Bus Station: Town Centre (1½ miles)
Club Shop: At the ground
Opening Times: Daily
Telephone Nº: (023) 9278-7822
Police Telephone Nº: (0845) 454545

GROUND INFORMATION

Away Supporters' Entrances & Sections: Martin Road End

ADMISSION INFO (2006/2007 PRICES)

Adult Standing/Seating: £9.00
Senior Citizen Standing/Seating: £6.00
Under-16s Standing/Seating: £4.00
Note: When accompanied by a paying adult, children under the age of 11 are admitted free of charge
Programme Price: £2.00

DISABLED INFORMATION

Wheelchairs: 12 spaces available in the Main Stand
Helpers: Admitted
Prices: Normal prices for disabled fans. Free for helpers
Disabled Toilets: Two available
Contact: (023) 9226-7276   (Bookings are necessary)

Travelling Supporters' Information:
Routes: From London or the North take the A27 from Chichester and exit at the B2149 turn-off for Havant. Take the 2nd exit off the dual carriageway into Bartons Road and then the 1st right into Martin Road for the ground; From the West: Take the M27 then the A27 to the Petersfield exit. Then as above.

HAYES FC

Founded: 1909
Former Names: Botwell Mission FC
Nickname: 'The Missioners'
Ground: Church Road, Hayes, Middlesex UB3 2LE
Record Attendance: 15,370 (10/2/51)
Pitch Size: 117 × 70 yards

Colours: Red & White striped shirts with Black shorts
Telephone Nº: (020) 8573-2075
Fax Number: (020) 8573-2075
Ground Capacity: 4,300
Seating Capacity: 500
Web site: www.hayesfc.net

GENERAL INFORMATION

Supporters Club: Lee Hermitage, c/o Hayes FC
Telephone Nº: (020) 8573-2075
Car Parking: 300 spaces available at the ground
Coach Parking: By arrangement
Nearest Railway Station: Hayes & Harlington (1 mile)
Nearest Bus Station: Hayes
Club Shop: At the ground
Opening Times: Matchdays only. Saturday matches from 2.00pm–5.00pm. Weekday matches from 6.45pm–9.30pm
Telephone Nº: (020) 8573-2075
Police Telephone Nº: (020) 8900-7212

GROUND INFORMATION

Away Supporters' Entrances & Sections:
Church Road End when segregated (not usual)

ADMISSION INFO (2006/2007 PRICES)

Adult Standing: £9.00
Adult Seating: £10.00
Child/Senior Citizen Standing: £5.00
Child/Senior Citizen Seating: £6.00
Programme Price: £2.00

DISABLED INFORMATION

Wheelchairs: Accommodated as necessary
Helpers: Admitted
Prices: £10.00 for the disabled but a helper is admitted free of charge with each paying disabled fan
Disabled Toilets: Available
Contact: (020) 8573-2075 (Bookings are not necessary)

Travelling Supporters' Information:
Routes: From the A40: Approaching London, take the Ruislip junction – turn right onto the B455 Ruislip Road to the White Hart Roundabout. Take the Hayes bypass to Uxbridge Road (A4020), turn right, then Church Road is ¾ mile on the left, opposite the Adam & Eve pub; From the M4: Exit at Junction 3 and take the A312 to Parkway towards Southall, then the Hayes bypass to Uxbridge Road (A4020). Turn left, then as above.

HISTON FC

Founded: 1904
Former Names: Histon Institute FC
Nickname: 'The Stutes'
Ground: The Glassworld Stadium, Bridge Road, Impington, Cambridge   CB4 9PH
Record Attendance: 6,400 (1956)
Pitch Size: 110 × 75 yards

Colours: Red shirts with Black shorts
Telephone Nº: (01223) 237373
Fax Number: (01223) 237373
Ground Capacity: 3,750
Seating Capacity: 350
Web site: www.histonfc.co.uk

GENERAL INFORMATION
Supporters Club: Yes
Telephone Nº: (01223) 846455 (Jenny Wells)
Car Parking: 250 spaces available at the ground
Coach Parking: For team coaches only
Nearest Railway Station: Cambridge (3 miles)
Nearest Bus Station: Cambridge (3 miles) (Service 107)
Club Shop: At the ground
Opening Times: Saturday matchdays 12.30pm – 6.00pm, Evening matches 6.00pm – 11.00pm
Telephone Nº: (01223) 237373

GROUND INFORMATION
Away Supporters' Entrances & Sections:
No usual segregation

ADMISSION INFO (2006/2007 PRICES)
Adult Standing: £9.00
Adult Seating: £9.00
Child Standing: £5.00
Child Seating: £5.00
Programme Price: £1.50

DISABLED INFORMATION
Wheelchairs: Accommodated
Helpers: Please contact the club for details
Prices: The disabled are charged concessionary prices
Disabled Toilets: Available
Contact: (01223) 237373   (Bookings are not necessary)

Travelling Supporters' Information:
Routes: Exit the M11 at Junction 14 and follow the A14 eastwards. Take the first exit onto the B1049 (signposted Histon & Cottenham). Turn left at the traffic lights at the top of the slip road and pass the Holiday Inn on the right. Continue over the bridge and the entrance to the ground is on the right.

LEWES FC

Founded: 1885
Former Names: None
Nickname: 'Rooks'
Ground: The Dripping Pan, Mountfield Road, Lewes BN7 1XN
Record Attendance: 2,500 (vs Newhaven 26/12/47)
Pitch Size: 110 × 72 yards

Colours: Red shirts with Black shorts
Telephone Nº: (01273) 472100
Fax Number: (01273) 472100
Ground Capacity: 3,000
Seating Capacity: 400
Web site: www.lewesfc.com

GENERAL INFORMATION
Supporters Club: c/o Club
Telephone Nº: (01273) 472100
Car Parking: At the ground
Coach Parking: At the ground
Nearest Railway Station: Lewes (adjacent)
Nearest Bus Station: Lewes (½ mile)
Club Shop: At the ground.
Opening Times: Matchdays only

GROUND INFORMATION
Away Supporters' Entrances & Sections:
No segregation

ADMISSION INFO (2006/2007 PRICES)
Adult Standing: £10.00
Adult Seating: £10.00
Junior Standing: £2.00 (Under-14s)
Junior Seating: £2.00 (Under-14s)
Senior Citizen/Under-16s Standing: £5.00
Senior Citizen/Under-16s Seating: £5.00
Programme Price: £2.00

DISABLED INFORMATION
Wheelchairs: Accommodated
Helpers: Admitted
Prices: Normal prices apply for the disabled and helpers
Disabled Toilets: Available
Contact: (01273) 472100

Travelling Supporters' Information:
Routes: From the North: Take the A26 or the A275 to Lewes and follow signs for the Railway Station. Pass the station on the left and take the next left. The ground is adjacent; From the South and West: Take the A27 to the A26 for the Town Centre. Then as above.

NEWPORT COUNTY FC

Founded: 1989
Former Names: Newport AFC
Nickname: 'The Exiles'
Ground: Newport Stadium, Stadium Way, Newport International Sports Village, Newport NP19 4PT
Record Attendance: 4,300 (31st March 2004)
Pitch Size: 112 × 72 yards

Colours: Amber shirts with Black shorts
Telephone Nº: (01633) 662262
Fax Number: (01633) 666107
Ground Capacity: 4,300
Seating Capacity: 1,236
Web site: www.newport-county.co.uk

GENERAL INFORMATION
Supporters Club: Bob Herrin, c/o Club
Telephone Nº: (01633) 274440
Car Parking: Space for 500 cars at the ground
Coach Parking: At the ground
Nearest Railway Station: Newport
Nearest Bus Station: Newport
Club Shop: At the ground
Opening Times: Matchdays only
Telephone Nº: (01633) 662262
Police Telephone Nº: (01633) 244999

GROUND INFORMATION
Away Supporters' Entrances & Sections:
No segregation unless specifically required by Police

ADMISSION INFO (2006/2007 PRICES)
Adult Standing: £8.00
Adult Seating: £8.00
Senior Citizen Standing: £5.50
Senior Citizen Seating: £5.50
Juniors: £1.00
Programme Price: £2.00

DISABLED INFORMATION
Wheelchairs: Accommodated
Helpers: Admitted
Prices: Normal prices for the disabled. Free for helpers
Disabled Toilets: Yes
Contact: (01633) 662262 (Bookings are not necessary)

Travelling Supporters' Information:
Routes: Exit the M4 at Junction 24 and take the exit at the roundabout, signposted 'Southern Distributor Road'. Go straight on at the first two roundabouts then turn left at the 3rd roundabout. Carry straight on over the next two roundabouts, pass the Velodrome then turn left between the two Carcraft buildings. Take the 1st turning on the left into the Stadium car park.

SALISBURY CITY FC

Founded: 1947
Former Names: Salisbury FC
Nickname: 'The Whites'
Ground: The Raymond McEnhill Stadium, Partridge Way, Old Sarum, Salisbury, Wiltshire   SP4 6PU
Record Attendance: 2,570   (14th November 1998)
Pitch Size: 115 × 76 yards

Colours: White shirts with Black shorts
Telephone Nº: (01722) 326454
Fax Number: (01722) 323100
Ground Capacity: 3,740
Seating Capacity: 450
Web site: www.salisburycity-fc.co.uk

GENERAL INFORMATION
Car Parking: At the ground
Coach Parking: At the ground
Nearest Railway Station: Salisbury (4 miles)
Nearest Bus Station: Salisbury
Club Shop: At the ground
Opening Times: Office Hours and Matchdays
Telephone Nº: (01722) 326454
Postal Sales: Yes
Police Telephone Nº: (01722) 411444

GROUND INFORMATION
Away Supporters' Entrances & Sections:
Portway End entrances and accommodation

ADMISSION INFO (2006/2007 PRICES)
Adult Standing: £8.00
Adult Seating: £10.00
Senior Citizen Standing: £5.00
Senior Citizen Seating: £7.00
Child Standing: Free of charge
Child Seating: £2.00
Programme Price: £2.00

DISABLED INFORMATION
Wheelchairs: Accommodated in a special area in the Main Stand
Helpers: Admitted
Prices: Normal prices apply
Disabled Toilets: Available
Contact: (01722) 326454   (Bookings are necessary)

Travelling Supporters' Information:
Routes: The Stadium well signposted and is situated off the main A345 Salisbury to Amesbury road on the northern edge of the City, 2 miles from the City Centre.

SUTTON UNITED FC

Founded: 1898
Former Names: Formed by the amalgamation of Sutton Guild Rovers FC and Sutton Association FC
Nickname: 'U's'
Ground: Borough Sports Ground, Gander Green Lane, Sutton, Surrey SM1 2EY
Record Attendance: 14,000 (1970)
Pitch Size: 110 × 72 yards

Colours: Chocolate and Amber striped shirts with Chocolate-coloured shorts
Telephone Nº: (020) 8644-4440
Fax Number: (020) 8644-5120
Ground Capacity: 7,032
Seating Capacity: 765
Web site: www.suttonunited.net

GENERAL INFORMATION

Supporters Club: Tony Cove, c/o Club
Telephone Nº: –
Car Parking: 150 spaces behind the Main Stand
Coach Parking: Space for 1 coach in the car park
Nearest Railway Station: West Sutton (adjacent)
Nearest Bus Station: Sutton
Club Shop: At the ground
Opening Times: Matchdays only
Telephone Nº: (020) 8644-4440
Police Telephone Nº: (020) 8680-1212

GROUND INFORMATION

Away Supporters' Entrances & Sections:
Collingwood Road entrances and accommodation

ADMISSION INFO (2006/2007 PRICES)

Adult Standing: £9.00
Adult Seating: £10.00
Child Standing: £3.00
Child Seating: £4.00
Senior Citizen Standing: £5.00
Senior Citizen Seating: £6.00
Programme Price: £2.00

DISABLED INFORMATION

Wheelchairs: 8 spaces are available under cover accommodated on the track perimeter
Helpers: Admitted
Prices: Normal prices apply
Disabled Toilets: Available alongside the Standing Terrace
Contact: (020) 8644-4440 (Bookings are necessary)

Travelling Supporters' Information:
Routes: Exit the M25 at Junction 8 (Reigate Hill) and travel North on the A217 for approximately 8 miles. Cross the A232 then turn right at the traffic lights (past Goose & Granit Public House) into Gander Green Lane. The ground is 300 yards on the left; From London: Gander Green Lane crosses the Sutton bypass 1 mile south of Rose Hill Roundabout. Avoid Sutton Town Centre, especially on Saturdays.

THURROCK FC

Founded: 1985
Former Names: Purfleet FC
Nickname: 'Fleet'
Ground: Thurrock Hotel, Ship Lane, Grays, Essex, RM19 1YN   **Telephone N°**: (01708) 865492
Record Attendance: 2,572 (1998)
Pitch Size: 113 × 72 yards

Colours: Yellow and Green shirts with Green shorts
Tel N°: (01708) 868901 (Hotel) or 865492 (Clubhouse)
Contact N°: (01708) 458301 (Secretary)
Fax Number: (01708) 868863
Ground Capacity: 4,200
Seating Capacity: 500
Web site: www.thurrockfc.com

GENERAL INFORMATION

Supporters Club: None
Car Parking: At the ground
Coach Parking: At the ground
Nearest Railway Station: Purfleet (2 miles)
Nearest Bus Station: Grays Town Centre
Club Shop: At the ground
Opening Times: Matchdays only
Telephone N°: (01708) 865492
Police Telephone N°: (01375) 391212

GROUND INFORMATION

Away Supporters' Entrances & Sections:
No usual segregation

ADMISSION INFO (2006/2007 PRICES)

Adult Standing: £9.00
Adult Seating: £9.00
Child Standing: £1.00
Child Seating: £1.00
Senior Citizen Standing: £5.00
Senior Citizen Seating: £5.00
Programme Price: £2.00

DISABLED INFORMATION

Wheelchairs: No special area but accommodated
Helpers: Admitted
Prices: Free for the disabled. Helpers pay normal prices
Disabled Toilets: Available in the Clubhouse
Contact: (01708) 865492   (Bookings are not necessary)

Travelling Supporters' Information:
Routes: Take the M25 or A13 to the Dartford Tunnel roundabout. The ground is then 50 yards on the right along Ship Lane.

WELLING UNITED FC

Founded: 1963
Former Names: None
Nickname: 'The Wings'
Ground: Park View Road Ground, Welling, Kent, DA16 1SY
Record Attendance: 4,020 (1989/90)
Pitch Size: 112 × 72 yards

Colours: Shirts are Red with White facings, Red shorts
Telephone Nº: (0208) 301-1196
Daytime Phone Nº: (0208) 301-1196
Fax Number: (0208) 301-5676
Ground Capacity: 4,000
Seating Capacity: 500
Web site: www.wellingunited.co.uk

GENERAL INFORMATION
Supporters Club: –
Car Parking: Street parking only
Coach Parking: Outside of the ground
Nearest Railway Station: Welling (¾ mile)
Nearest Bus Station: Bexleyheath
Club Shop: At the ground
Opening Times: Matchdays only
Telephone Nº: (0208) 301-1196
Police Telephone Nº: (0208) 304-3161

GROUND INFORMATION
Away Supporters' Entrances & Sections:
Accommodation in the Danson Park End

ADMISSION INFO (2006/2007 PRICES)
Adult Standing: £10.00
Adult Seating: £11.00
Senior Citizen/Child Standing: £6.00
Senior Citizen/Child Seating: £7.00
Under-12s: £4.00
Programme Price: £2.00

DISABLED INFORMATION
Wheelchairs: Accommodated at the side of the Main Stand
Helpers: Admitted
Prices: £6.00 for the disabled. Helpers pay normal prices
Disabled Toilets: Yes
Contact: (0208) 301-1196 (Bookings are not necessary)

Travelling Supporters' Information:
Routes: Take the A2 (Rochester Way) from London, then the A221 Northwards (Danson Road) to Bexleyheath. At the end turn left towards Welling along Park View Road and the ground is on the left.

WESTON-SUPER-MARE FC

Founded: 1899
Former Names: Christ Church Old Boys FC
Nickname: 'Seagulls'
Ground: Woodspring Stadium, Winterstoke Road, Weston-Super-Mare   BS24 9AA
Record Attendance: 2,623   (vs Woking in F.A. Cup)
Pitch Size: 110 × 70 yards

Colours: White shirts with Blue shorts
Telephone Nº: (01934) 621618
Fax Number: (01934) 622704
Ground Capacity: 3,071
Seating Capacity: 278
Web site: www.westonsupermarefc.co.uk

GENERAL INFORMATION

Supporters Club: Joe Varian, 336 Milton Road, Weston-Super-Mare
Telephone Nº: (01934) 627929
Car Parking: 140 spaces available at the ground
Coach Parking: At the ground
Nearest Railway Station: Weston-Super-Mare (1½ miles)
Nearest Bus Station: Weston-Super-Mare (1½ miles)
Club Shop: At the ground
Opening Times: Matchdays only
Telephone Nº: (01934) 621618
Police Telephone Nº: (01275) 818181

GROUND INFORMATION

Away Supporters' Entrances & Sections:
No usual segregation

ADMISSION INFO (2006/2007 PRICES)

Adult Standing/Seating: £8.50
Senior Citizen/Student Standing/Seating: £5.50
Child Standing/Seating: £5.50
Under-5s: £3.00
Programme Price: £1.50

DISABLED INFORMATION

Wheelchairs: Accommodated in a special disabled section
Helpers: Admitted
Prices: Normal prices apply
Disabled Toilets: One available
Contact: (01934) 621618   (Bookings are not necessary)

Travelling Supporters' Information:
Routes: Exit the M5 at Junction 21 and follow the dual carriageway (A370) to the 4th roundabout (Asda Winterstoke). Turn left, go over the mini-roundabout and continue for 800 yards. The ground is on the right.

YEADING FC

Founded: 1960
Former Names: None
Nickname: 'The Ding'
Ground: The Warren, Beaconsfield Road, Hayes, UB4 0SL
Record Attendance: 3,000 (1990)
Pitch Size: 115 × 72 yards

Colours: Red & Black striped shirts with Black shorts
Telephone Nº: (020) 8848-7362
Fax Number: (020) 8756-1200
Ground Capacity: 3,500
Seating Capacity: 250
Web site: www.yeadingfc.co.uk

GENERAL INFORMATION
Supporters Club: –
Car Parking: At the ground
Coach Parking: At the ground
Nearest Railway Station: Hayes (2 miles)
Nearest Bus Station: Uxbridge (2½ miles)
Club Shop: None
Opening Times: –

GROUND INFORMATION
Away Supporters' Entrances & Sections:
No usual segregation

ADMISSION INFO (2006/2007 PRICES)
Adult Standing: £8.00
Adult Seating: £8.00
Senior Citizen/Under-16s Standing: £5.00
Senior Citizen/Under-16s Seating: £5.00
Note: Under-12s are admitted for £1.00 with a paying adult
Programme Price: £1.50

DISABLED INFORMATION
Wheelchairs: Accommodated
Helpers: Admitted
Prices: Normal prices apply
Disabled Toilets: None
Contact: (020) 8848-7362

Travelling Supporters' Information:
Routes: Exit the M4 at Junction 4 and take the A312 past Hayes & Harlington Station. Cross the Grand Union Canal and continue to the Uxbridge Road crossroads. Turn right along Uxbridge Road towards Southall for about ¾ mile then turn right at the traffic lights into Springfield Road then left into Beaconsfield Road. The ground is on the right at the bottom of the road.
Note: Do not approach from the Southall end of Beaconsfield Road – no access to the ground due to the Grand Union Canal!

Football Conference National 2005/2006 Season	Accrington Stanley	Aldershot Town	Altrincham	Burton Albion	Cambridge United	Canvey Island	Crawley Town	Dagenham & Redbridge	Exeter City	Forest Green Rovers	Gravesend & Northfleet	Grays Athletic	Halifax Town	Hereford United	Kidderminster Harriers	Morecambe	Scarborough	Southport	Stevenage Borough	Tamworth	Woking	York City
Accrington Stanley		3-2	1-0	2-1	1-0	1-0	4-2	1-0	1-2	2-0	1-1	2-3	1-1	2-1	2-0	2-0	1-0	4-0	1-1	2-1	2-1	2-1
Aldershot Town	1-4		0-2	1-1	1-3	2-2	3-2	3-1	1-0	2-1	3-2	0-3	3-1	0-1	1-0	2-0	0-1	2-0	2-2	0-2	1-1	2-1
Altrincham	0-1	5-1		1-2	2-1	0-1	1-1	0-5	1-1	2-1	2-2	0-2	1-2	0-1	3-0	2-0	1-1	1-0	1-1	2-0	0-4	0-3
Burton Albion	0-2	1-2	1-0		2-0	1-2	3-1	2-2	2-0	1-0	0-0	1-1	1-2	0-1	1-0	0-4	2-1	0-0	3-1	1-1	1-1	0-0
Cambridge United	3-1	0-2	4-0	2-2		3-1	2-1	1-2	2-1	2-2	1-1	1-1	2-1	0-2	2-2	2-1	2-1	1-0	2-1	0-2	2-0
Canvey Island	0-2	2-1	1-1	0-2	1-1		1-0	1-2	1-1	1-1	1-2	2-1	0-1	1-1	2-1	3-3	1-0	2-1	1-1	1-2	0-2	1-1
Crawley Town	0-1	2-0	2-0	1-1	1-0	3-1		0-0	0-2	1-0	1-2	1-3	2-2	0-2	2-0	1-3	2-0	2-0	1-2	3-0	2-2	0-1
Dagenham & Redbridge	1-2	2-0	2-4	3-1	1-0	2-2	0-3		2-2	1-1	1-2	1-2	1-0	0-1	3-0	3-1	0-2	3-1	2-2	2-1	1-3	0-2
Exeter City	1-3	4-0	3-1	1-2	4-0	0-2	4-0	3-1		0-0	1-0	1-2	4-2	1-2	1-0	2-0	1-1	5-0	0-2	3-0	1-1	1-3
Forest Green Rovers	1-1	4-2	5-0	1-0	1-0	1-2	2-2	0-3	0-0		0-0	1-2	2-2	2-2	0-0	1-0	5-1	1-2	2-0	1-3	0-3	1-2
Gravesend & Northfleet	1-3	0-3	2-0	0-1	0-0	2-0	1-1	1-3	0-2	2-0		1-3	4-0	1-2	1-2	1-0	0-0	2-1	0-2	2-0	2-0	2-2
Grays Athletic	1-2	2-1	1-1	2-3	5-3	1-2	1-0	0-4	3-0	2-2	6-1		1-1	2-2	2-2	1-2	5-0	1-1	2-2	5-0	2-2	1-1
Halifax Town	2-2	1-1	2-0	1-0	1-0	0-2	2-2	3-0	2-0	1-0	2-0	2-1		2-1	0-0	0-0	1-0	2-1	1-1	4-0	1-0	1-0
Hereford United	2-2	2-1	0-0	2-0	3-0	1-1	2-1	1-1	0-2	1-1	1-1	0-2	1-0		0-1	1-0	4-0	1-1	2-0	1-0	4-0	1-0
Kidderminster Harriers	2-0	1-4	1-1	0-1	1-0	3-2	1-0	3-1	1-2	1-3	0-2	0-5	0-1	1-1		1-0	2-1	1-1	0-0	0-1	2-1	0-0
Morecambe	3-2	5-2	2-0	3-1	0-1	1-0	3-0	2-0	2-2	3-2	3-0	3-0	1-0	2-2	2-0		0-3	0-0	4-1	0-0	3-1	2-0
Scarborough	2-2	2-2	1-2	3-0	1-2	1-2	1-2	0-1	0-1	1-0	3-1	2-7	2-0	0-1	1-1	0-1		0-1	1-1	0-0	1-1	2-2
Southport	2-0	0-1	1-1	3-2	2-2	2-0	0-2	1-2	0-3	3-1	1-0	1-4	0-2	1-2	1-4	0-3	0-2		3-2	1-1	1-0	1-4
Stevenage Borough	3-1	2-1	3-0	2-3	3-1	3-0	2-1	2-1	2-0	2-1	2-0	0-1	1-0	0-0	3-1	1-0	2-0	0-1		3-1	1-1	1-1
Tamworth	1-2	2-1	1-1	1-1	1-1	1-0	0-0	2-2	1-1	0-0	1-0	2-2	1-2	0-1	1-1	0-3	0-1	0-0	2-0		0-1	0-3
Woking	0-1	1-2	3-1	2-2	0-1	1-1	0-0	0-0	1-0	2-1	1-3	1-1	2-2	1-1	0-1	0-1	4-0	1-0	3-2	5-0		2-0
York City	2-4	3-2	5-0	0-1	1-0	2-1	0-0	1-1	4-2	5-1	1-0	1-2	0-2	1-3	2-2	1-1	3-1	0-0	0-1	2-1	2-1	

Nationwide Conference National

Season 2005/2006

Team	P	W	D	L	F	A	Pts
Accrington Stanley	42	28	7	7	76	45	91
Hereford United	42	22	14	6	59	33	80
Grays Athletic	42	21	13	8	94	55	76
Halifax Town	42	21	12	9	55	40	75
Morecambe	42	22	8	12	68	41	74
Stevenage Borough	42	19	12	11	62	47	69
Exeter City	42	18	9	15	65	48	63
York City	42	17	12	13	63	48	63
Burton Albion	42	16	12	14	50	52	60
Dagenham & Redbridge	42	16	10	16	63	59	58
Woking	42	14	14	14	58	47	56
Cambridge United	42	15	10	17	51	57	55
Aldershot Town	42	16	6	20	61	74	54
Canvey Island	42	13	12	17	47	58	51
Kidderminster Harriers	42	13	11	18	39	55	50
Gravesend & Northfleet	42	13	10	19	45	57	49
Crawley Town	42	12	11	19	48	55	47
Southport	42	10	10	22	36	68	40
Forest Green Rovers	42	8	14	20	49	62	38
Tamworth	42	8	14	20	32	63	38
Scarborough	42	9	10	23	40	66	37
Altrincham	42	10	11	21	40	71	23

Altrincham had 18 points deducted for fielding an ineligible player but were not relegated after Canvey Island withdrew from the League and Scarborough were relegated for a breach of the rules.

Promotion Play-offs

Halifax Town 3   Grays Athletic 2
Morecambe 1   Hereford United 1

Grays Athletic 2   Halifax Town 2
Halifax Town won 5-4 on aggregate

Hereford United 3   Morecambe .... 2 (aet)
Hereford United won 4-3 on aggregate

Halifax Town 2   Hereford United .... 3 (aet)

Promoted: Accrington Stanley and Hereford United
Relegated: Scarborough

	Alfreton Town	Barrow	Droylsden	Gainsborough Trinity	Harrogate Town	Hednesford Town	Hinckley United	Hucknall Town	Hyde United	Kettering Town	Lancaster City	Leigh RMI	Moor Green	Northwich Victoria	Nuneaton Borough	Redditch United	Stafford Rangers	Stalybridge Celtic	Vauxhall Motors	Worcester City	Workington	Worksop Town
Alfreton Town	■	2-1	1-3	1-2	4-1	3-2	1-1	1-1	2-0	1-1	0-2	1-1	1-1	2-4	1-0	2-1	2-1	0-0	1-2	1-0	1-3	2-1
Barrow	2-2	■	2-0	3-1	3-1	3-1	2-5	2-0	2-2	0-1	1-4	3-1	2-2	1-1	0-3	1-1	1-1	4-2	0-2	0-2	6-1	1-0
Droylsden	1-0	2-2	■	1-2	2-1	1-1	3-1	2-3	1-0	3-1	6-1	4-1	3-0	4-3	2-2	2-1	2-1	1-0	4-0	3-0	2-3	3-1
Gainsborough Trinity	2-2	3-2	2-2	■	0-2	1-1	1-2	3-2	0-3	0-2	1-0	2-1	2-2	1-2	1-2	2-2	1-1	1-0	1-1	0-1	0-0	2-0
Harrogate Town	1-0	2-1	1-1	2-0	■	2-3	2-1	1-0	1-0	1-1	3-1	3-0	3-0	0-2	2-0	1-1	0-2	1-0	2-1	4-1	1-1	2-0
Hednesford Town	1-0	0-3	0-1	1-1	0-4	■	3-4	1-1	0-2	2-2	1-0	1-3	1-2	1-4	0-0	1-1	0-2	1-1	0-1	0-4	0-0	2-1
Hinckley United	2-2	1-0	1-1	1-0	1-3	1-2	■	3-1	2-1	1-1	3-3	5-1	1-2	1-3	0-1	1-1	0-1	1-1	2-1	1-3	0-0	3-0
Hucknall Town	1-0	2-1	2-0	4-1	4-1	2-2	0-2	■	1-3	1-1	0-0	2-2	2-2	3-2	0-1	4-1	0-2	2-1	1-2	1-2	1-0	0-0
Hyde United	2-3	2-2	2-2	2-0	3-1	4-2	0-1	0-0	■	3-0	2-4	3-3	3-2	1-3	1-0	1-3	1-3	1-3	2-3	4-0	1-1	1-1
Kettering Town	1-0	1-3	1-0	1-2	0-2	4-0	2-2	0-0	3-2	■	2-0	4-0	0-3	2-0	3-0	4-0	0-1	4-1	1-0	2-1	2-1	1-0
Lancaster City	2-2	3-0	2-2	2-3	2-1	1-0	2-2	0-1	1-3	0-1	■	2-0	3-3	1-1	1-0	1-1	2-2	1-0	0-0	0-1		2-1
Leigh RMI	0-0	1-1	0-1	0-0	3-1	0-0	1-0	2-1	1-1	0-2	1-2	■	1-3	2-1	1-0	2-1	1-3	2-1	1-1	1-4	0-1	0-1
Moor Green	0-0	1-1	1-1	1-1	2-2	1-2	1-1	2-4	1-2	1-1	3-1	4-1	■	1-2	0-4	2-1	0-1	1-1	2-1	1-1	1-4	1-0
Northwich Victoria	1-1	2-0	2-1	2-0	3-0	8-0	2-0	2-0	1-2	3-1	3-2	1-0	1-1	■	2-2	5-1	3-1	1-0	3-1	0-1	4-1	4-1
Nuneaton Borough	1-0	2-1	2-2	3-1	4-0	3-2	2-0	2-2	1-0	2-2	3-0	3-1	2-2	1-2	■	2-1	1-1	0-0	3-2	0-0	3-1	3-1
Redditch United	1-0	2-1	4-1	1-1	1-3	1-2	1-1	1-1	1-1	2-1	0-1	1-2	0-1	1-2	3-0	■	0-1	1-4	3-0	2-2	3-6	0-3
Stafford Rangers	1-0	3-1	0-0	3-0	0-1	1-1	2-3	2-0	1-0	1-3	3-0	0-0	1-3	2-0	2-0	3-0	■	1-0	3-0	1-1	2-2	4-2
Stalybridge Celtic	3-0	2-1	1-1	1-0	3-1	3-0	1-1	2-1	1-2	2-0	2-1	6-1	4-1	3-3	2-0	5-1	2-3	■	2-1	2-3	2-1	2-1
Vauxhall Motors	3-1	0-1	2-4	1-2	0-2	0-0	0-1	0-2	0-2	1-1	1-0	4-4	1-2	0-3	1-2	1-2	1-3	4-2	■	1-0	2-1	5-2
Worcester City	2-2	1-0	1-2	2-1	2-0	6-2	0-0	0-1	2-2	2-0	2-0	2-0	0-2	0-1	0-1	2-2	1-1	0-1	0-0	■	1-1	1-1
Workington	2-0	0-0	2-1	2-0	2-4	2-0	1-1	1-1	1-0	3-2	1-1	0-0	1-4	5-2	0-2	1-2	0-1	1-2	1-2	2-2	■	1-2
Worksop Town	1-1	2-1	3-2	1-1	1-0	3-3	0-0	2-1	1-1	2-1	2-0	3-3	0-2	1-2	0-4	1-1	0-1	2-1	1-1	0-3	1-2	■

Nationwide Conference North

Season 2005/2006

Team	P	W	D	L	F	A	Pts
Northwich Victoria	42	29	5	8	97	49	92
Stafford Rangers	42	25	10	7	68	34	85
Nuneaton Borough	42	22	11	9	68	43	77
Droylsden	42	20	12	10	80	56	72
Harrogate Town	42	22	5	15	66	56	71
Kettering Town	42	19	10	13	63	49	67
Stalybridge Celtic	42	19	9	14	74	54	66
Worcester City	42	16	14	12	58	46	62
Moor Green	42	15	16	11	67	64	61
Hinckley United	42	14	16	12	60	55	58
Hyde United (P)	42	15	11	16	68	61	56
Hucknall Town	42	14	13	15	56	55	55
Workington (P)	42	14	13	15	60	62	55
Barrow	42	12	11	19	62	67	47
Lancaster City	42	12	11	19	52	66	47
Gainsborough Trinity	42	11	13	18	45	65	46
Alfreton Town	42	10	15	17	46	58	45
Vauxhall Motors	42	12	7	23	50	71	43
Worksop Town	42	10	11	21	46	71	41
Redditch United	42	9	12	21	53	78	39
Leigh RMI	42	9	13	20	45	79	39
Hednesford Town	42	7	14	21	42	87	35

Leigh RMI had 1 point deducted.

Promotion Play-offs North

Nuneaton Borough .... 0 Droylsden 1
Stafford Rangers .... 1 Harrogate Town 0

Droylsden .... 1 Stafford Rangers .... 1 (aet)
Stafford Rangers won 5-3 on penalties

Promoted from Conference North: Northwich Victoria and Stafford Rangers

Football Conference South 2005/2006 Season	Basingstoke Town	Bishop's Stortford	Bognor Regis Town	Cambridge City	Carshalton Athletic	Dorchester Town	Eastbourne Borough	Eastleigh	Farnborough Town	Havant & Waterlooville	Hayes	Histon	Lewes	Maidenhead United	Newport County	St. Albans City	Sutton United	Thurrock	Welling United	Weston-super-Mare	Weymouth	Yeading
Basingstoke Town		1-1	2-3	0-5	2-1	2-0	2-2	0-1	0-1	2-1	1-1	0-1	1-5	0-1	1-0	1-1	2-0	0-3	2-2	2-1	0-3	0-4
Bishop's Stortford	1-1		2-1	1-3	3-3	5-2	0-1	4-1	1-1	1-3	1-0	5-0	0-3	1-0	0-1	1-3	2-1	2-2	1-1	2-3	0-2	2-1
Bognor Regis Town	2-1	2-2		4-2	1-1	1-1	2-1	2-0	0-1	0-1	1-1	3-1	2-2	8-1	1-1	2-1	0-0	0-1	0-0	0-1	0-2	0-2
Cambridge City	1-0	1-1	2-0		0-0	1-2	2-3	2-1	0-2	0-0	3-1	3-1	0-2	3-0	0-2	4-3	3-0	6-0	0-0	3-0	1-3	0-2
Carshalton Athletic	1-2	0-0	1-1	0-2		3-1	2-2	1-3	2-2	1-3	1-2	0-0	2-2	0-1	1-0	0-2	0-0	0-0	1-0	1-1	2-1	2-2
Dorchester Town	2-1	1-3	3-5	1-0	2-0		3-0	1-3	1-1	1-1	2-2	0-3	2-2	1-3	2-2	1-4	0-5	2-0	0-3	1-2	2-0	4-0
Eastbourne Borough	2-3	1-1	0-0	1-1	1-1	1-1		0-1	0-1	2-2	0-0	1-1	3-1	3-3	2-0	1-1	2-1	0-0	1-1	1-3	0-2	2-1
Eastleigh	0-3	0-1	1-0	1-1	3-1	1-2	2-1		2-0	2-6	2-1	1-2	2-0	2-1	2-0	0-2	2-0	3-0	1-3	4-1	2-0	0-3
Farnborough Town	1-0	3-0	2-1	0-3	4-0	0-1	2-3	1-0		4-1	0-0	0-2	2-2	3-1	2-1	0-0	2-1	0-0	1-0	5-0	0-1	1-0
Havant & Waterlooville	2-0	2-2	1-0	1-1	1-1	1-0	1-0	2-1	1-0		1-1	3-1	1-0	2-1	1-2	0-1	0-1	1-2	0-0	3-2	2-1	3-0
Hayes	1-2	2-0	1-2	2-0	1-2	0-1	0-2	1-0	0-1	1-2		2-1	2-2	2-1	3-2	0-1	2-1	0-1	1-3	4-1	1-2	0-1
Histon	2-0	3-2	2-2	1-0	0-1	4-1	3-1	1-0	3-6	3-1	2-3		1-1	3-0	2-3	0-5	3-0	3-1	1-1	1-1	2-1	1-0
Lewes	3-0	2-1	1-1	2-2	2-1	3-2	1-0	1-2	6-2	0-2	2-1	0-3		2-2	1-0	0-2	2-0	0-0	2-1	5-2	2-3	1-0
Maidenhead United	0-0	2-2	1-2	0-5	0-2	2-3	2-6	2-2	1-2	3-1	2-1	1-4	0-1		1-1	0-4	2-0	1-3	2-4	2-4	0-0	1-2
Newport County	2-0	1-0	1-0	0-2	4-1	0-2	1-1	0-2	1-2	2-3	1-0	0-1	2-3	3-0		1-3	1-0	3-4	2-2	2-2	0-3	1-3
St. Albans City	3-1	3-0	2-0	2-4	3-0	2-0	5-0	2-4	2-2	2-0	1-0	1-0	4-0	1-0	2-0		3-1	3-2	3-1	1-2	4-0	5-2
Sutton United	0-1	1-1	1-0	3-2	1-1	1-0	2-0	0-3	1-0	1-1	2-1	1-1	1-5	4-1	1-1	4-0		1-1	2-1	1-2	0-3	0-0
Thurrock	4-1	2-1	3-0	0-3	2-1	0-1	1-0	3-1	0-2	0-2	1-1	1-2	2-3	1-2	4-2	2-1	5-3		1-1	0-1	1-2	0-1
Welling United	3-2	0-0	2-0	1-1	2-0	4-3	1-2	2-1	1-0	2-2	1-0	1-1	2-1	3-3	1-1	3-1	0-0	1-1		1-0	1-0	0-1
Weston-super-Mare	4-3	0-1	2-2	1-3	2-0	0-4	1-0	1-4	1-1	1-3	1-1	1-4	1-2	1-1	2-1	3-1	2-3	0-5	0-1		1-3	0-3
Weymouth	1-1	3-1	2-0	1-1	4-0	1-0	2-1	2-0	1-2	1-0	5-1	1-0	2-0	4-0	4-0	3-2	3-1	2-0	2-1	2-1		1-1
Yeading	0-4	0-0	0-3	1-2	3-4	0-1	1-1	2-2	0-3	2-0	2-3	1-0	0-3	0-2	1-2	2-2	0-2	1-1	1-0	1-2	0-1	

Nationwide Conference South

Season 2005/2006

Weymouth	42	30	4	8	80	34	90
St. Albans City	42	27	5	10	94	47	86
Farnborough Town	42	23	9	10	65	41	78
Lewes	42	21	10	11	78	57	73
Histon	42	21	10	11	70	56	71
Havant & Waterlooville	42	21	10	11	64	48	70
Cambridge City	42	20	10	12	78	46	67
Eastleigh	42	21	3	18	65	58	66
Welling United	42	16	17	9	58	44	65
Thurrock	42	16	10	16	60	60	58
Dorchester Town	42	16	7	19	60	72	55
Bognor Regis Town	42	12	13	17	54	55	49
Sutton United	42	13	10	19	48	61	49
Weston-super-Mare	42	14	7	21	57	88	49
Bishop's Stortford	42	11	15	16	55	63	48
Yeading	42	13	8	21	47	62	47
Eastbourne Borough	42	10	16	16	51	61	46
Newport County	42	12	8	22	50	67	44
Basingstoke Town	42	12	8	22	47	72	44
Hayes	42	11	9	22	47	60	42
Carshalton Athletic	42	8	16	18	42	68	40
Maidenhead United	42	8	9	25	49	99	31

Weymouth had 4 points deducted.
Havant & Waterlooville and Cambridge City had 3 points deducted.
Maidenhead United had 2 points deducted.

Promotion Play-offs South

Farnborough Town 0   Histon 3
St. Albans City qualified for the final after Lewes withdrew

Histon 0   St. Albans City 2

Promoted from Conference South:

Weymouth and St. Albans City

Northern Premier League Division One — 2005/2006 Season

	Bamber Bridge	Belper Town	Bishop Auckland	Bridlington Town	Brigg Town	Chorley	Clitheroe	Colwyn Bay	Eastwood Town	Fleetwood Town	Goole	Gresley Rovers	Kendal Town	Kidsgrove Athletic	Mossley	Ossett Albion	Rossendale United	Shepshed Dynamo	Spalding United	Stocksbridge PS	Warrington Town	Woodley Sports
Bamber Bridge	■	0-1	7-2	1-1	3-4	3-1	2-2	2-1	3-1	2-1	1-0	1-1	0-5	2-4	1-2	0-0	0-1	2-1	4-0	1-1	2-1	1-1
Belper Town	1-0	■	2-1	2-3	1-1	3-1	2-0	2-1	2-1	1-4	2-0	2-1	3-4	0-0	4-0	1-4	0-1	0-1	2-2	0-1	1-1	1-0
Bishop Auckland	1-1	1-3	■	2-1	0-3	1-4	1-2	0-1	0-1	1-3	0-2	1-2	2-2	2-1	1-2	1-2	1-1	0-4	0-2	1-4	2-3	0-3
Bridlington Town	2-0	2-1	1-0	■	3-1	4-1	1-0	0-0	2-3	1-1	3-1	2-2	1-2	1-1	2-1	2-1	1-2	1-0	1-0	1-1	1-1	0-2
Brigg Town	3-2	1-2	2-0	3-2	■	1-0	2-2	1-1	2-2	3-1	1-0	2-1	2-1	2-3	0-1	2-3	2-2	0-1	3-1	0-0	3-2	1-2
Chorley	0-1	1-0	2-1	2-2	1-2	■	1-1	0-1	1-0	0-1	2-2	1-1	1-2	1-2	3-0	2-3	1-2	1-1	1-1	3-0	1-4	
Clitheroe	1-0	0-2	4-1	2-0	2-2	0-1	■	1-0	0-3	1-0	1-0	3-3	0-3	2-2	3-2	4-2	2-0	1-1	2-1	0-1	2-3	3-2
Colwyn Bay	1-1	0-1	2-0	1-3	0-0	1-2	0-0	■	0-0	2-0	4-1	6-0	0-1	4-3	3-0	2-0	0-4	2-0	3-0	1-1	3-0	2-1
Eastwood Town	1-1	2-0	2-0	0-3	2-0	0-4	3-1	4-1	■	0-1	3-3	2-3	3-3	2-1	2-2	3-2	4-0	1-1	0-0	1-1	3-3	4-0
Fleetwood Town	0-0	2-0	3-2	2-3	5-1	2-1	4-0	2-1	3-2	■	0-1	1-1	1-2	0-2	1-1	2-2	2-2	1-0	2-1	1-1	1-0	2-0
Goole	3-3	1-0	1-0	2-2	2-2	2-2	1-0	3-0	0-3	3-3	■	2-3	2-4	1-1	0-0	1-4	1-1	0-5	1-6	0-4	2-3	1-4
Gresley Rovers	3-1	3-1	3-1	2-1	3-2	2-1	3-1	3-2	2-0	0-2	4-0	■	0-1	0-0	3-1	3-1	1-0	0-0	3-0	1-1	2-3	2-5
Kendal Town	2-0	2-2	3-3	2-1	1-4	1-2	1-4	0-0	1-1	2-1	3-1	0-3	■	4-0	1-1	0-1	4-0	1-3	3-0	1-1	3-1	2-1
Kidsgrove Athletic	0-2	1-0	3-0	3-2	1-4	1-0	5-0	6-0	0-0	0-3	3-3	0-1	0-2	■	2-3	1-3	2-1	2-3	3-0	0-3	3-3	2-1
Mossley	1-1	4-2	2-1	6-1	1-0	2-1	1-0	1-2	4-0	1-3	3-0	3-1	5-2	2-1	■	7-0	2-1	2-3	3-1	2-0	1-1	2-2
Ossett Albion	3-2	0-2	2-2	5-2	1-2	1-2	2-1	1-0	0-0	1-2	0-1	2-1	1-2	0-1	0-2	■	1-0	1-1	1-2	1-0	1-1	2-1
Rossendale United	1-1	2-2	3-0	5-0	1-1	0-1	2-1	2-1	1-0	0-1	2-2	1-4	3-2	1-1	0-0	0-1	■	2-4	3-3	0-0	2-2	2-3
Shepshed Dynamo	0-5	0-1	0-0	0-0	1-1	1-0	5-0	0-0	0-2	4-0	0-4	1-2	0-3	2-1	2-1	1-1	2-2	■	0-0	0-1	2-1	1-2
Spalding United	1-1	0-0	2-1	2-0	1-1	1-2	1-2	2-3	0-0	0-4	0-2	4-3	3-0	2-1	0-4	1-1	0-0	2-2	■	2-2	2-2	1-0
Stocksbridge PS	1-1	4-1	4-2	1-0	3-0	1-3	4-0	1-1	3-1	1-2	1-2	2-1	0-1	2-0	2-3	1-0	2-3	3-1	0-0	■	2-1	0-0
Warrington Town	0-3	0-0	4-2	3-0	1-1	2-1	1-0	1-2	1-2	2-4	2-1	0-0	0-1	3-2	1-1	2-0	0-0	2-2	1-2	2-2	■	1-3
Woodley Sports	3-1	3-0	0-2	1-2	2-2	0-2	2-2	2-1	4-1	0-0	2-1	2-1	2-2	2-1	5-0	0-0	2-0	5-1	3-0	4-2	4-1	■

Unibond League Premier Division

Season 2005/2006

Team	P	W	D	L	F	A	Pts
Blyth Spartans	42	26	11	5	79	32	89
Frickley Athletic	42	26	8	8	72	36	86
Marine	42	23	12	7	61	25	81
Farsley Celtic	42	23	10	9	84	34	79
North Ferriby United	42	21	10	11	77	54	73
Whitby Town	42	18	10	14	60	59	64
Burscough	42	19	6	17	64	64	63
Witton Albion	42	17	9	16	68	55	60
Matlock Town	42	16	11	15	60	55	59
AFC Telford United	42	14	17	11	54	52	59
Ossett Town	42	17	7	18	57	61	58
Leek Town	42	14	14	14	50	53	56
Prescot Cables	42	15	8	19	49	60	53
Guiseley	42	14	9	19	45	58	51
Ashton United	42	13	10	19	62	63	49
Ilkeston Town	42	12	13	17	48	51	49
Gateshead	42	12	10	20	52	77	46
Radcliffe Borough	42	12	8	22	54	62	44
Lincoln United	42	10	14	18	44	64	44
Wakefield Emley	42	11	9	22	38	69	42
Bradford Park Avenue	42	10	9	23	64	86	39
Runcorn FC Halton	42	6	11	25	36	108	29

Promotion Play-offs

Marine 0   Farsley Celtic 1
Frickley Athletic 0   North Ferriby United ..... 0 (aet)
North Ferriby United won 4-2 on penalties

Farsley Celtic 2   North Ferriby United ..... 1 (aet)

Promoted: Blyth Spartans and Farsley Celtic

Southern League Premier Division 2005/2006 Season	Aylesbury United	Banbury United	Bath City	Bedford Town	Chesham United	Cheshunt	Chippenham Town	Cirencester Town	Evesham United	Gloucester City	Grantham Town	Halesowen Town	Hitchin Town	King's Lynn	Mangotsfield United	Merthyr Tydfil	Northwood	Rugby Town	Salisbury City	Team Bath	Tiverton Town	Yate Town
Aylesbury United		2-0	1-5	1-2	0-1	1-0	1-1	1-0	2-2	0-1	0-2	2-1	1-3	1-0	1-1	0-2	3-0	1-1	1-3	1-2	0-5	3-0
Banbury United	2-1		2-3	3-2	0-1	1-1	4-2	2-1	3-2	1-0	1-1	1-0	2-2	4-2	2-4	4-2	0-1	2-1	1-2	1-1	3-1	1-1
Bath City	3-2	0-3		1-1	1-0	2-0	0-2	3-0	2-0	0-0	2-0	0-0	2-1	1-1	1-2	2-0	3-0	1-0	0-2	3-1	1-0	1-2
Bedford Town	2-1	3-2	1-0		2-3	1-1	2-1	2-1	1-1	5-3	1-1	0-0	0-2	3-2	1-0	0-1	4-0	1-1	1-0	1-1	3-0	2-0
Chesham United	1-1	1-1	0-1	0-3		4-2	0-1	0-2	0-2	0-2	2-2	0-2	0-0	1-0	2-0	2-2	3-1	1-2	1-4	0-2	3-3	2-5
Cheshunt	0-1	2-0	1-0	0-3	4-1		1-1	1-2	1-0	1-1	3-2	2-3	1-2	0-1	2-2	3-3	5-2	2-3	0-1	2-1	1-0	2-3
Chippenham Town	1-1	1-0	2-0	1-2	3-0	1-1		2-0	2-0	3-0	1-0	0-0	2-2	1-1	3-1	2-1	3-1	4-0	2-1	4-2	0-1	4-2
Cirencester Town	2-1	1-3	1-2	5-1	0-1	0-2	1-1		0-1	0-1	0-1	2-1	2-1	0-2	0-3	1-1	0-0	1-2	2-5	1-0	2-1	1-3
Evesham United	2-0	0-0	1-2	1-1	3-1	0-1	0-2	0-4		0-0	0-2	1-1	2-0	1-1	2-3	1-2	4-0	3-0	2-2	0-1	1-1	0-1
Gloucester City	1-1	1-1	0-2	0-0	3-1	3-2	0-1	0-1	1-1		4-1	1-0	1-0	1-2	1-3	1-1	4-1	5-2	1-2	3-0	4-5	2-0
Grantham Town	2-0	2-3	0-3	3-0	0-0	0-1	1-1	0-1	1-1	2-1		1-1	1-1	0-1	1-2	0-0	2-0	2-2	1-0	0-1	1-1	2-0
Halesowen Town	1-1	2-2	2-1	1-1	1-0	1-1	1-2	1-1	2-0	1-0	0-2		1-1	0-0	1-3	4-1	3-2	0-1	1-3	4-2		7-2
Hitchin Town	3-2	3-0	2-2	1-4	1-1	4-1	3-3	1-3	2-2	2-2	0-2	1-0		0-5	0-0	1-2	4-2	1-0	0-3	2-1	3-2	4-3
King's Lynn	1-1	2-0	0-2	1-0	2-0	2-0	3-1	2-1	2-1	4-0	3-1	0-1	3-0		1-1	0-3	3-2	1-1	1-3	4-2	4-1	1-0
Mangotsfield United	0-0	1-2	0-2	0-2	4-3	2-1	1-2	3-0	2-2	5-4	0-1	1-1	1-0	1-3		3-0	1-3	1-3	0-0	3-3	1-1	0-3
Merthyr Tydfil	2-4	1-0	0-0	1-3	1-4	2-0	4-0	3-1	3-0	2-2	2-1	2-3	1-2	0-1	1-0		0-1	1-1	0-1	1-0	1-1	3-0
Northwood	2-1	2-1	0-3	2-3	1-1	3-1	2-1	3-0	1-2	0-1	0-2	3-0	0-0	0-1	3-5	2-3		0-0	2-2	1-1	2-4	3-2
Rugby Town	4-0	3-0	1-2	5-2	3-0	1-5	0-0	1-2	1-3	0-1	0-2	0-0	4-1	0-3	2-2	1-0	1-2		1-3	1-0	3-1	0-0
Salisbury City	3-0	1-3	0-0	1-0	6-0	5-0	2-1	3-0	1-0	2-0	3-0	0-1	3-0	1-0	2-0	3-0	3-0			0-1	1-0	3-1
Team Bath	1-1	2-2	0-4	1-2	2-0	0-1	2-0	4-2	2-1	1-0	1-2	0-2	1-0	1-3	0-1	2-3	2-3	1-3	1-2		0-2	5-3
Tiverton Town	1-1	0-0	1-2	0-1	4-0	1-1	0-2	0-4	3-0	1-0	3-1	0-0	6-2	1-2	2-3	2-0	4-1	2-2	0-1	2-0		3-2
Yate Town	3-0	0-3	1-1	4-0	5-2	4-1	1-2	3-1	1-1	3-1	3-1	2-1	2-1	3-2	2-2	3-2	1-0	1-0	1-0	0-3	2-1	

Southern League Premier Division

Season 2005/2006

Team	P	W	D	L	F	A	Pts
Salisbury City	42	30	5	7	83	27	95
Bath City	42	25	8	9	66	33	83
King's Lynn	42	25	7	10	73	41	82
Chippenham Town	42	22	11	9	69	45	77
Bedford Town	42	22	10	10	69	53	76
Yate Town	42	21	5	16	78	74	68
Banbury United	42	17	11	14	66	61	62
Halesowen Town	42	15	15	12	54	45	60
Merthyr Tydfil	42	17	9	16	62	58	60
Mangotsfield United	42	15	13	14	67	67	58
Grantham Town	42	15	11	16	49	49	56
Tiverton Town	42	14	10	18	69	65	52
Gloucester City	42	14	10	18	57	60	52
Hitchin Town	42	13	12	17	59	76	51
Rugby Town	42	13	11	18	58	66	50
Cheshunt	42	13	9	20	57	70	48
Team Bath	42	14	6	22	55	68	48
Cirencester Town	42	14	4	24	49	68	46
Northwood	42	12	6	24	53	88	42
Evesham United	42	9	14	19	46	58	41
Aylesbury United	42	9	12	21	43	69	39
Chesham United	42	9	9	24	43	84	36

Promotion Play-offs

King's Lynn 1   Chippenham Town 3
Bath City 0   Bedford Town 1

Chippenham Town 2   Bedford Town 3

Promoted: Salisbury City and Bedford Town

Isthmian League Premier Division 2005/2006 Season	AFC Wimbledon	Billericay Town	Braintree Town	Bromley	Chelmsford City	East Thurrock United	Fisher Athletic	Folkestone Invicta	Hampton & Richmond	Harrow Borough	Hendon	Heybridge Swifts	Leyton	Maldon Town	Margate	Redbridge	Slough Town	Staines Town	Walton & Hersham	Wealdstone	Windsor & Eton	Worthing
AFC Wimbledon		1-1	1-1	1-1	0-1	3-2	1-0	4-1	0-4	2-1	2-1	1-0	0-0	3-0	1-2	5-0	2-2	1-1	2-1	1-1	1-1	1-2
Billericay Town	2-1		1-1	2-2	4-2	1-3	1-3	2-0	1-2	3-1	1-0	1-2	2-2	2-3	4-1	1-0	3-1	1-1	0-2	2-0	3-0	1-1
Braintree Town	0-0	2-0		3-1	2-1	1-0	3-2	3-0	2-1	3-0	1-0	3-0	1-1	1-1	1-0	2-0	2-1	3-1	3-1	2-0	3-0	4-2
Bromley	2-0	1-0	1-1		1-1	1-1	1-2	3-3	2-0	1-1	3-1	2-1	1-2	2-1	2-2	1-0	2-3	1-1	1-0	1-1	4-1	1-2
Chelmsford City	1-0	2-1	0-2	3-2		2-4	0-2	0-1	3-3	3-0	3-0	0-2	1-1	1-2	1-0	2-1	2-0	4-4	1-1	0-0	2-1	1-0
East Thurrock United	1-1	0-3	1-3	1-0	3-0		2-5	0-2	1-2	3-2	3-0	0-4	1-3	1-1	3-1	2-0	3-2	0-2	1-0	2-0	0-2	5-1
Fisher Athletic	0-1	0-2	1-1	0-0	3-3	1-2		0-0	4-3	4-1	0-1	2-0	4-1	1-1	2-1	3-1	1-2	2-1	2-0	2-1	2-0	2-2
Folkestone Invicta	1-0	1-0	0-0	1-0	1-1	1-0	0-1		1-2	2-1	1-2	0-2	2-2	2-0	1-1	1-0	3-0	0-2	3-1	5-2	1-0	1-2
Hampton & Richmond	2-1	0-1	0-1	0-0	3-0	1-0	0-3	3-1		1-3	3-1	0-5	4-2	1-2	0-1	3-1	3-2	2-1	2-0	3-0	4-0	1-2
Harrow Borough	1-2	1-1	1-0	2-0	2-1	5-4	0-2	5-0	0-2		1-1	1-2	3-3	1-1	0-0	0-0	2-1	1-4	1-2	1-2	2-1	2-2
Hendon	0-1	2-2	1-2	2-1	0-0	0-0	1-2	0-0	0-2	2-1		0-1	4-0	1-1	1-2	2-0	1-1	1-2	1-1	0-3	1-2	2-2
Heybridge Swifts	1-1	0-0	0-3	1-0	2-0	0-1	1-2	2-0	2-1	2-1	3-0		1-0	2-0	2-0	2-0	1-0	4-2	1-3	2-0	1-1	
Leyton	1-2	1-3	0-1	0-1	5-1	1-2	3-4	1-1	1-1	0-1	2-0	0-1		4-2	0-2	4-0	1-2	0-2	0-1	1-2	2-1	1-0
Maldon Town	0-2	0-2	2-3	0-2	0-1	3-2	0-3	1-0	1-2	1-4	2-2	0-1	0-2		1-1	2-1	0-2	2-2	1-2	2-4	1-2	2-0
Margate	0-1	1-1	1-1	1-1	0-1	2-1	1-1	1-1	3-2	0-0	4-2	1-2	0-1	1-0		0-0	2-2	2-5	2-4	1-0	1-1	0-0
Redbridge	0-3	0-5	0-1	3-2	1-2	0-1	0-5	0-2	0-2	0-1	0-2	1-2	0-4	0-0	3-1		1-4	1-2	1-3	2-3	1-1	3-2
Slough Town	0-2	0-2	2-1	2-2	0-1	1-2	0-4	2-0	0-1	5-2	0-2	1-0	0-0	4-1	2-2	3-2		1-2	0-2	3-2	3-3	0-3
Staines Town	0-3	1-2	1-1	1-2	3-0	1-0	2-0	2-2	0-1	1-0	2-0	5-1	2-3	1-1	2-1	2-2	2-1		2-1	1-3	1-0	0-1
Walton & Hersham	0-2	0-0	3-2	0-1	2-2	1-0	0-1	0-3	2-0	3-1	1-0	2-1	2-0	3-0	1-1	2-1	0-1	0-2		1-0	3-2	2-3
Wealdstone	1-5	1-1	2-3	1-2	1-2	0-2	1-2	1-2	1-2	4-1	4-5	3-4	1-0	0-2	0-4	6-1	2-2	1-2	1-3		4-2	2-1
Windsor & Eton	0-4	1-0	0-1	0-1	1-2	0-0	1-4	1-0	1-3	0-1	1-1	3-4	2-0	0-0	0-1	1-0	0-3	1-2	1-1	0-3		2-1
Worthing	0-2	2-4	2-0	1-2	1-3	1-0	4-0	1-0	2-1	3-0	1-1	4-1	0-3	2-1	1-1	5-1	4-2	2-2	0-0	3-1	2-1	

Rymans League Premier Division

Season 2005/2006

Braintree Town	42	28	10	4	74	32	94
Heybridge Swifts	42	28	3	11	70	46	87
Fisher Athletic	42	26	7	9	84	46	85
AFC Wimbledon	42	22	11	9	67	36	77
Hampton & Richmond	42	24	3	15	73	54	75
Staines Town	42	20	10	12	74	56	70
Billericay Town	42	19	12	11	69	45	69
Worthing	42	19	10	13	71	60	67
Walton & Hersham	42	19	7	16	55	50	64
Chelmsford City	42	18	10	14	57	62	64
Bromley	42	16	14	12	57	49	62
East Thurrock United	42	18	5	19	60	60	59
Folkestone Invicta	42	16	10	16	47	51	58
Margate	42	11	17	14	49	55	50
Leyton	42	13	9	20	58	61	48
Harrow Borough	42	13	9	20	56	73	48
Slough Town	42	13	8	21	63	75	47
Wealdstone	42	13	5	24	68	82	44
Hendon	42	9	12	21	44	64	39
Maldon Town	42	8	11	23	41	73	35
Windsor & Eton	42	8	8	26	37	75	32
Redbridge	42	3	5	34	28	97	14

Promotion Play-offs

Heybridge Swifts 1   Hampton & Richmond .. 1 (aet)
Hampton & Richmond Borough won 4-2 on penalties
Fisher Athletic 2   AFC Wimbledon 1

Fisher Athletic 3   Hampton & Richmond 0

Promoted: Braintree Town and Fisher Athletic

LDV Trophy 2005/2006

Round 1	Barnsley	2	Doncaster Rovers	5	
Round 1	Blackpool	4	Wrexham	3	(aet)
Round 1	Cambridge United	3	Chester City	0	
Round 1	Grimsby Town	1	Morecambe	1	(aet)
	Morecambe won on penalties				
Round 1	Halifax Town	6	Bury	1	
Round 1	Kidderminster Harriers	2	Darlington	1	
Round 1	Macclesfield Town	2	Chesterfield	0	
Round 1	Mansfield Town	0	Hereford United	1	
Round 1	Oldham Athletic	1	Carlisle United	1	(aet)
	Carlisle United won on penalties				
Round 1	Rochdale	3	Stockport County	1	
Round 1	Rotherham United	3	Accrington Stanley	3	(aet)
	Rotherham United won on penalties				
Round 1	Scunthorpe United	1	Hartlepool United	0	
Round 1	Tranmere Rovers	2	Lincoln City	1	
Round 1	Barnet	3	Bristol City	2	
Round 1	Bournemouth	4	Aldershot Town	1	
Round 1	Brentford	1	Oxford United	1	(aet)
	Oxford United won on penalties				
Round 1	Gillingham	2	Crawley Town	0	(aet)
Round 1	Leyton Orient	2	Yeovil Town	0	
Round 1	Milton Keynes Dons	3	Exeter City	2	
Round 1	Northampton Town	5	Notts County	2	
Round 1	Peterborough United	2	Bristol Rovers	1	(aet)
Round 1	Rushden & Diamonds	1	Southend United	0	
Round 1	Shrewsbury Town	0	Cheltenham Town	2	
Round 1	Swindon Town	2	Stevenage Borough	0	
Round 1	Torquay United	1	Swansea City	3	
Round 1	Woking	3	Nottingham Forest	2	
Round 1	Wycombe Wanderers	2	Dagenham& Redbridge	1	(aet)
Round 1	Boston United	2	Huddersfield Town	1	
Round 2	Woking	1	Cheltenham Town	5	(aet)
Round 2	Cambridge United	3	Doncaster Rovers	2	
Round 2	Carlisle United	2	Blackpool	1	
Round 2	Halifax Town	1	Scunthorpe United	3	
Round 2	Hereford United	2	Port Vale	1	
Round 2	Morecambe	0	Bradford City	1	
Round 2	Rotherham United	1	Macclesfield Town	2	
Round 2	Tranmere Rovers	3	Rochdale	2	
Round 2	Barnet	0	MiltonKeynes Dons	3	
Round 2	Gillingham	2	Wycombe Wanderers	2	(aet)
	Wycombe Wanderers won on penalties				
Round 2	Peterborough United	2	Swindon Town	1	
Round 2	Swansea City	4	Rushden & Diamonds	0	
Round 2	Walsall	1	Bournemouth	0	
Round 2	Boston United	0	Kidderminster Harriers	3	
Round 2	Colchester United	3	Northampton Town	2	(aet)
Round 2	Oxford United	1	Leyton Orient	0	

Round 3	Macclesfield	4	Cambridge United	2	
Round 3	Swansea City	3	Peterborough United	1	(aet)
Round 3	Hereford United	2	Scunthorpe United	0	
Round 3	Kidderminster Harriers	2	Bradford City	1	
Round 3	Tranmere Rovers	0	Carlisle United	0	(aet)
	Carlisle United won on penalties				
Round 3	Cheltenham Town	2	Oxford United	1	
Round 3	MiltonKeynes Dons	1	Colchester United	2	
Round 3	Walsall	3	Wycombe Wanderers	2	
Semi-Final North	Carlisle United	1	Kidderminster Harriers	0	
Semi-Final North	Macclesfield Town	2	Hereford United	0	
Semi-Final South	Cheltenham Town	0	Colchester United	1	
Semi-Final South	Swansea City	2	Walsall	2	(aet)
	Swansea City won on penalties				

Southern Final

1st leg	Swansea City	1	Colchester United	0	
2nd leg	Colchester United	1	Swansea City	2	
	Swansea City won 3-1 on aggregate				

Northern Final

1st leg	Carlisle United	2	Macclesfield Town	1	
2nd leg	Macclesfield Town	3	Carlisle United	2	
	Aggregate score 4-4. Carlisle United won on the away goals rule				

FINAL	Swansea City	2	Carlisle United	1	

F.A. Trophy 2005/2006

Qualifying 1	AFC Wimbledon	1	King's Lynn	0	
Qualifying 1	Ashford Town	0	Bromley	2	
Qualifying 1	Bamber Bridge	2	Grantham Town	2	
Qualifying 1	Banstead Athletic	1	Redbridge	2	
Qualifying 1	Barton Rovers	3	Potters Bar Town	2	
Qualifying 1	Bashley	0	Margate	3	
Qualifying 1	Bedford Town	3	Bracknell Town	0	
Qualifying 1	Billericay Town	1	Wingate & Finchley	0	
Qualifying 1	Blyth Spartans	2	Belper Town	0	(aet)
Qualifying 1	Boreham Wood	1	Ilford	0	
Qualifying 1	Brackley Town	1	Banbury United	1	
Qualifying 1	Bradford Park Avenue	1	Gateshead	1	
Qualifying 1	Braintree Town	4	Great Wakering Rovers	2	
Qualifying 1	Brigg Town	0	Matlock Town	1	
Qualifying 1	Bromsgrove Rovers	3	Beaconsfield SYCOB	2	
Qualifying 1	Burnham	2	Yate Town	0	
Qualifying 1	Burscough	3	Leek Town	3	
Qualifying 1	Chelmsford City	6	Horsham	0	
Qualifying 1	Cinderford Town	1	Chippenham Town	1	
Qualifying 1	Cirencester Town	2	Gloucester City	0	
Qualifying 1	Clevedon Town	2	Taunton Town	1	
Qualifying 1	Clitheroe	3	Spalding United	1	
Qualifying 1	Corinthian Casuals	1	Stamford	4	
Qualifying 1	Dover Athletic	1	Dartford	1	
Qualifying 1	Dulwich Hamlet	1	Barking & East Ham United	1	
Qualifying 1	Dunstable Town	2	Bath City	2	
Qualifying 1	Enfield	1	Fleet Town	2	
Qualifying 1	Enfield Town	3	Berkhamsted Town	0	
Qualifying 1	Evesham United	0	Solihull Borough	2	
Qualifying 1	Farsley Celtic	2	Runcorn FC Halton	0	
Qualifying 1	Fisher Athletic	4	Hendon	2	
Qualifying 1	Folkestone Invicta	1	Whyteleafe	1	
Qualifying 1	Gresley Rovers	2	Ilkeston Town	2	
Qualifying 1	Guiseley	3	Chorley	1	
Qualifying 1	Halesowen Town	0	Willenhall Town	0	
Qualifying 1	Hampton & Richmond Borough	0	Newport (IOW)	2	
Qualifying 1	Hastings United	0	Corby Town	0	
Qualifying 1	Hemel Hempstead	1	Swindon Supermarine	1	
Qualifying 1	Heybridge Swifts	3	Walton & Hersham	0	
Qualifying 1	Kidsgrove Athletic	3	Ashton United	1	
Qualifying 1	Kingstonian	2	Aveley	2	
Qualifying 1	Leatherhead	0	East Thurrock United	1	
Qualifying 1	Leighton Town	2	Rugby Town	1	
Qualifying 1	Leyton	1	Arlesey Town	0	
Qualifying 1	Lincoln United	2	Colwyn Bay	1	
Qualifying 1	Lymington & New Milton	0	Worthing	4	
Qualifying 1	Marlow	1	Ashford Town (Middx)	2	
Qualifying 1	Merthyr Tydfil	0	Rushall Olympic	3	
Qualifying 1	Metropolitan Police	4	Maldon Town	1	
Qualifying 1	Mossley	3	Shepshed Dynamo	2	
Qualifying 1	North Ferriby United	1	Prescot Cables	1	
Qualifying 1	Northwood	2	Ramsgate	4	
Qualifying 1	Ossett Albion	0	Kendal Town	4	
Qualifying 1	Ossett Town	1	Stocksbridge Park Steels	1	

Qualifying 1	Paulton Rovers	1	Salisbury City	1
Qualifying 1	Radcliffe Borough	1	Marine	2
Qualifying 1	Rossendale United	0	Woodley Sports	1
Qualifying 1	Rothwell Town	3	Molesey	1
Qualifying 1	Sittingbourne	3	Chatham Town	0
Qualifying 1	Slough Town	1	Croydon Athletic	3
Qualifying 1	Staines Town	2	Wivenhoe Town	0
Qualifying 1	Stourport Swifts	0	Bedworth United	1
Qualifying 1	Sutton Coldfield Town	2	Chesham United	1
Qualifying 1	Team Bath	0	Hitchin Town	1
Qualifying 1	Thame United	0	Aylesbury United	5
Qualifying 1	Tiverton Town	0	Mangotsfield United	0
Qualifying 1	Tonbridge Angels	1	Cheshunt	0
Qualifying 1	Tooting & Mitcham United	1	Wealdstone	2
Qualifying 1	Wakefield & Emley	0	Fleetwood Town	5
Qualifying 1	Waltham Forest	0	Burgess Hill Town	1
Qualifying 1	Walton Casuals	0	Harlow Town	1
Qualifying 1	Warrington Town	1	Frickley Athletic	1
Qualifying 1	Whitby Town	4	Eastwood Town	2
Qualifying 1	Windsor & Eton	1	Uxbridge	2
Qualifying 1	Witton Albion	1	AFC Telford United	1
Replay	AFC Telford United	2	Witton Albion	1
Replay	Aveley	0	Kingstonian	1
Replay	Banbury United	3	Brackley Town	0
Replay	Barking & East Ham United	2	Dulwich Hamlet	0
Replay	Bath City	5	Dunstable Town	0
Replay	Chippenham Town	3	Cinderford Town	1
Replay	Corby Town	2	Hastings United	0
Replay	Dartford	3	Dover Athletic	2
Replay	Frickley Athletic	1	Warrington Town	1	(aet)
	Warrington Town won on penalties			
Replay	Gateshead	4	Bradford Park Avenue	3
Replay	Grantham Town	3	Bamber Bridge	0
Replay	Ilkeston Town	2	Gresley Rovers	3
Replay	Leek Town	1	Burscough	3
Replay	Mangotsfield United	1	Tiverton Town	2
Replay	Prescot Cables	2	North Ferriby United	2	(aet)
	Prescot Cables won on penalties			
Replay	Salisbury City	3	Paulton Rovers	1	(aet)
Replay	Stocksbridge Park Steels	2	Ossett Town	2	(aet)
	Ossett Town won on penalties			
Replay	Swindon Supermarine	0	Hemel Hempstead	1
Replay	Whyteleafe	1	Folkestone Invicta	2
Replay	Willenhall Town	2	Halesowen Town	3	(aet)
Qualifying 2	AFC Telford United	1	Goole AFC	1
Qualifying 2	Banbury United	2	Cirencester Town	2
Qualifying 2	Barking & East Ham United	4	Burgess Hill Town	1
Qualifying 2	Bath City	2	Bromsgrove Rovers	0
Qualifying 2	Bedworth United	2	Sutton Coldfield Town	5
Qualifying 2	Bishop Auckland	1	Woodley Sports	3
Qualifying 2	Blyth Spartans	2	Whitby Town	0
Qualifying 2	Boreham Wood	4	Bromley	1
Qualifying 2	Bridlington Town	2	Warrington Town	2
Qualifying 2	Burnham	3	Leighton Town	5
Qualifying 2	Burscough	1	Fleetwood Town	2
Qualifying 2	Chelmsford City	0	Braintree Town	2

Qualifying 2	Cray Wanderers	4	Staines Town	3	
Qualifying 2	Croydon Athletic	2	Rothwell Town	2	
Qualifying 2	East Thurrock United	2	Leyton	1	
Qualifying 2	Enfield Town	1	Redbridge	1	
Qualifying 2	Fisher Athletic	1	Uxbridge	2	
Qualifying 2	Fleet Town	0	Kingstonian	1	
Qualifying 2	Folkestone Invicta	5	Wealdstone	3	
Qualifying 2	Gateshead	1	Kidsgrove Athletic	0	
	Gateshead were disqualified for fielding an ineligible player				
Qualifying 2	Grantham Town	2	Lincoln United	1	
Qualifying 2	Gresley Rovers	1	Mossley	4	
Qualifying 2	Guiseley	2	Kendal Town	2	
Qualifying 2	Halesowen Town	2	Aylesbury United	0	
Qualifying 2	Harlow Town	2	Barton Rovers	1	
Qualifying 2	Harrow Borough	4	Metropolitan Police	2	
Qualifying 2	Hemel Hempstead	2	Chippenham Town	3	
Qualifying 2	Heybridge Swifts	2	Billericay Town	1	
Qualifying 2	Hitchin Town	1	Bedford Town	2	
Qualifying 2	Margate	0	Dartford	1	
Qualifying 2	Marine	2	Matlock Town	1	
Qualifying 2	Ossett Town	2	Clitheroe	2	
Qualifying 2	Prescot Cables	1	Farsley Celtic	2	
Qualifying 2	Ramsgate	1	AFC Wimbledon	1	
Qualifying 2	Rushall Olympic	3	Ashford Town (Middx)	4	
Qualifying 2	Salisbury City	2	Clevedon Town	1	
Qualifying 2	Sittingbourne	1	Corby Town	0	
Qualifying 2	Solihull Borough	3	Tiverton Town	1	
Qualifying 2	Tonbridge Angels	2	Newport (IOW)	1	
Qualifying 2	Worthing	1	Stamford	1	
Replay	AFC Wimbledon	2	Ramsgate	1	
Replay	Cirencester Town	3	Banbury United	4	(aet)
Replay	Clitheroe	1	Ossett Town	1	(aet)
	Clitheroe won on penalties				
Replay	Goole AFC	0	AFC Telford United	1	
Replay	Kendal Town	4	Guiseley	0	
Replay	Redbridge	2	Enfield Town	1	
Replay	Rothwell Town	0	Croydon Athletic	1	
Replay	Stamford	2	Worthing	0	
Replay	Warrington Town	1	Bridlington Town	0	
Qualifying 3	Ashford Town (Middx)	2	Bognor Regis Town	3	
Qualifying 3	Barking & East Ham United	2	Croydon Athletic	1	
Qualifying 3	Basingstoke Town	0	Welling United	2	
Qualifying 3	Bath City	1	Yeading	2	
Qualifying 3	Boreham Wood	3	Stamford	1	
Qualifying 3	Braintree Town	0	Hayes	1	
Qualifying 3	Chippenham Town	0	Carshalton Athletic	2	
Qualifying 3	Clitheroe	2	Woodley Sports	1	
Qualifying 3	Cray Wanderers	1	Kingstonian	1	
Qualifying 3	Dartford	0	AFC Wimbledon	0	
Qualifying 3	Droylsden	4	Grantham Town	0	
Qualifying 3	Eastbourne Borough	0	Thurrock	3	
Qualifying 3	Farnborough Town	2	Banbury United	0	
Qualifying 3	Farsley Celtic	3	Nuneaton Borough	1	
Qualifying 3	Fleetwood Town	1	Alfreton Town	3	
Qualifying 3	Harlow Town	2	Folkestone Invicta	1	
Qualifying 3	Hednesford Town	1	Moor Green	1	

Qualifying 3	Heybridge Swifts	0	St Albans City	1	
Qualifying 3	Hinckley United	2	Histon	2	
Qualifying 3	Hucknall Town	0	Northwich Victoria	0	
Qualifying 3	Hyde United	1	Stalybridge Celtic	5	
Qualifying 3	Kettering Town	1	Gainsborough Trinity	0	
Qualifying 3	Lancaster City	0	Workington	0	
Qualifying 3	Leigh RMI	1	Stafford Rangers	4	
Qualifying 3	Leighton Town	1	Eastleigh	1	
Qualifying 3	Lewes	2	Dorchester Town	2	
Qualifying 3	Maidenhead United	2	Bishop's Stortford	2	
Qualifying 3	Marine	0	Blyth Spartans	1	
Qualifying 3	Redbridge	1	Harrow Borough	1	
Qualifying 3	Redditch United	1	Barrow	1	
Qualifying 3	Salisbury City	3	Newport County	0	
Qualifying 3	Sittingbourne	1	Cambridge City	3	
Qualifying 3	Solihull Borough	1	Harrogate Town	0	
Qualifying 3	Sutton Coldfield Town	1	Halesowen Town	1	
Qualifying 3	Tonbridge Angels	0	East Thurrock United	0	
Qualifying 3	Uxbridge	2	Sutton United	2	
Qualifying 3	Vauxhall Motors (Cheshire)	2	Mossley	1	
Qualifying 3	Warrington Town	4	Kidsgrove Athletic	0	
Qualifying 3	Weston Super Mare	4	Bedford Town	0	
Qualifying 3	Weymouth	2	Havant & Waterlooville	1	
Qualifying 3	Worcester City	1	Kendal Town	0	
Qualifying 3	Worksop Town	1	AFC Telford United	1	
Replay	AFC Telford United	1	Worksop Town	2	
Replay	AFC Wimbledon	2	Dartford	0	
Replay	Barrow	2	Redditch United	0	
Replay	Bishop's Stortford	2	Maidenhead United	1	(aet)
Replay	Dorchester Town	3	Lewes	1	
Replay	East Thurrock United	3	Tonbridge Angels	0	
Replay	Eastleigh	1	Leighton Town	2	(aet)
Replay	Halesowen Town	3	Sutton Coldfield Town	0	
Replay	Harrow Borough	2	Redbridge	3	(aet)
Replay	Histon	2	Hinckley United	1	
Replay	Kingstonian	3	Cray Wanderers	1	
Replay	Moor Green	2	Hednesford Town	4	
Replay	Northwich Victoria	2	Hucknall Town	1	
Replay	Sutton United	0	Uxbridge	1	
Replay	Workington	1	Lancaster City	2	
Round 1	AFC Wimbledon	2	St Albans City	3	
Round 1	Accrington Stanley	2	Altrincham	0	
Round 1	Aldershot Town	1	Grays Athletic	1	
Round 1	Alfreton Town	1	Histon	1	
Round 1	Barrow	2	Clitheroe	1	
Round 1	Bognor Regis Town	1	Hereford United	7	
Round 1	Boreham Wood	1	Leighton Town	0	
Round 1	Burton Albion	0	Worksop Town	1	
Round 1	Canvey Island	4	Kingstonian	1	
Round 1	Dagenham & Redbridge	2	Thurrock	0	
Round 1	Dorchester Town	3	Cambridge United	2	
Round 1	East Thurrock United	0	Gravesend & Northfleet	2	
Round 1	Exeter City	2	Bishop's Stortford	1	
Round 1	Farnborough Town	0	Cambridge City	2	
Round 1	Halesowen Town	1	Tamworth	2	
Round 1	Halifax Town	0	Southport	0	

Round 1	Kettering Town	2	Farsley Celtic	1	
Round 1	Kidderminster Harriers	4	Scarborough	0	
Round 1	Salisbury City	1	Harlow Town	0	
Round 1	Solihull Borough	2	Hednesford Town	1	
Round 1	Stafford Rangers	4	Lancaster City	2	
Round 1	Stalybridge Celtic	1	Droylsden	0	
Round 1	Stevenage Borough	0	Crawley Town	2	
Round 1	Uxbridge	1	Woking	2	
Round 1	Vauxhall Motors (Cheshire)	0	Morecambe	4	
Round 1	Warrington Town	1	Blyth Spartans	2	
Round 1	Welling United	4	Redbridge	1	
Round 1	Weston Super Mare	3	Barking & East Ham United	2	
Round 1	Weymouth	0	Forest Green Rovers	1	
Round 1	Worcester City	1	Hayes	0	
Round 1	Yeading	1	Carshalton Athletic	2	
Round 1	York City	1	Northwich Victoria	2	
Replay	Grays Athletic	1	Aldershot Town	0	(aet)
Replay	Histon	2	Alfreton Town	1	
Replay	Southport	0	Halifax Town	1	
Round 2	Barrow	1	Cambridge City	2	
Round 2	Blyth Spartans	1	Welling United	3	
Round 2	Boreham Wood	3	Gravesend & Northfleet	1	
Round 2	Canvey Island	0	Salisbury City	1	
Round 2	Carshalton Athletic	2	Accrington Stanley	2	
Round 2	Crawley Town	3	Worcester City	1	
Round 2	Dagenham & Redbridge	2	Kettering Town	1	
Round 2	Exeter City	3	Histon	2	
Round 2	Forest Green Rovers	3	Dorchester Town	1	
Round 2	Halifax Town	0	Hereford United	1	
Round 2	Kidderminster Harriers	0	Grays Athletic	1	
Round 2	Stafford Rangers	1	Morecambe	0	
Round 2	Stalybridge Celtic	1	Solihull Borough	0	
Round 2	Tamworth	1	St Albans City	0	
Round 2	Weston Super Mare	1	Worksop Town	1	
Round 2	Woking	1	Northwich Victoria	1	
Round 2	Worksop Town	2	Weston Super Mare	1	
Replay	Accrington Stanley	2	Carshalton Athletic	0	
Replay	Northwich Victoria	1	Woking	2	(aet)
Round 3	Accrington Stanley	1	Worksop Town	1	
Round 3	Crawley Town	0	Boreham Wood	2	
Round 3	Exeter City	1	Cambridge City	0	
Round 3	Hereford United	0	Grays Athletic	1	
Round 3	Salisbury City	0	Stalybridge Celtic	0	
Round 3	Stafford Rangers	2	Forest Green Rovers	1	
Round 3	Tamworth	0	Dagenham & Redbridge	0	
Round 3	Woking	3	Welling United	2	
Replay	Dagenham & Redbridge	3	Tamworth	0	
Replay	Stalybridge Celtic	0	Salisbury City	1	
Replay	Worksop Town	1	Accrington Stanley	1	(aet)
	Worksop Town won on penalties				
Round 4	Exeter City	3	Salisbury City	1	
Round 4	Grays Athletic	1	Dagenham & Redbridge	1	
Round 4	Woking	1	Stafford Rangers	1	
Round 4	Worksop Town	0	Boreham Wood	1	

| Replay | Dagenham & Redbridge | 2 | Grays Athletic | 4 |
| Replay | Stafford Rangers | 2 | Woking | 4 |

SEMI-FINALS

1st leg	Boreham Wood	0	Woking	1
2nd leg	Woking	2	Boreham Wood	0
	Woking won 3-0 on penalties			

1st leg	Exeter City	2	Grays Athletic	1
2nd leg	Grays Athletic	2	Exeter City	0
	Grays Athletic won 3-2 on aggregate			

| FINAL | Grays Athletic | 2 | Woking | 0 |

F.A. Vase 2005/2006

Round 1	AFC Wallingford	1	Wisbech Town	4	
Round 1	Abingdon Town	0	Egham Town	2	
Round 1	Alnwick Town	1	Glasshoughton Welfare	3	
Round 1	Armthorpe Welfare	0	Norton & Stockton Ancients	1	
Round 1	Arundel	4	Croydon	2	
Round 1	Ashington	3	Thornaby	3	(aet)
Round 1	Ashville	3	Penrith	1	(aet)
Round 1	Aylesbury Vale	1	Bicester Town	2	
Round 1	Barrow Town	4	Borrowash Victoria	3	(aet)
Round 1	Biddulph Victoria	2	Castle Vale	1	
Round 1	Bournemouth	4	Odd Down	1	
Round 1	Bristol Manor Farm	2	Highworth Town	3	
Round 1	Brockenhurst	2	Abingdon United	1	
Round 1	Bromyard Town	0	Chasetown	1	
Round 1	Carterton	1	Hungerford Town	0	
Round 1	Chard Town	1	Dawlish Town	1	(aet)
Round 1	Chessington & Hook United	1	Horsham YMCA	0	
Round 1	Clevedon United	2	St Blazey	4	(aet)
Round 1	Coalville Town	7	Dudley Town	0	
Round 1	Cockfosters	0	Ipswich Wanderers	3	
Round 1	Cogenhoe United	0	AFC Hornchurch	1	
Round 1	Concord Rangers	2	Halstead Town	0	(aet)
Round 1	Consett	0	Cammell Laird	1	
Round 1	Cove	0	VCD Athletic	2	
Round 1	Cradley Town	4	Newark Town	2	
Round 1	Crook Town	2	Winsford United	0	
Round 1	Daisy Hill	0	Nelson	1	
Round 1	Darlington Railway Athletic	2	Dunston Federation Brewery	2	(aet)
Round 1	Darwen	2	Harrogate Railway	4	
Round 1	Deeping Rangers	0	Buxton	4	
Round 1	Devizes Town	0	Pewsey Vale	0	(aet)
Round 1	Dorking	4	Hamble ASSC	1	
Round 1	East Grinstead Town	3	Rye & Iden United	5	
Round 1	Erith & Belvedere	1	Hillingdon Borough	5	
Round 1	Erith Town	2	Whitehawk	0	
Round 1	Felixstowe & Walton United	3	Chalfont St Peter	3	(aet)
Round 1	Ford Sports Daventry	2	Sutton Town	1	
Round 1	Friar Lane & Epworth	5	Shirebrook Town	1	
Round 1	Glossop North End	6	Romulus	4	
Round 1	Godalming Town	1	Hassocks	4	

Round 1	Gorleston	1	Raunds Town	0	
Round 1	Greenwich Borough	1	Colliers Wood United	3	
Round 1	Hallen	0	Slimbridge	1	
Round 1	Hanwell Town	4	Colney Heath	1	
Round 1	Heanor Town	0	Arnold Town	2	
Round 1	Herne Bay	4	Epsom & Ewell	2	(aet)
Round 1	Highfield Rangers	2	St Andrews	0	
Round 1	Holbeach United	0	Leamington	2	
Round 1	Hullbridge Sports	0	Mildenhall Town	8	
Round 1	Kingsbury Town	2	Haringey Borough	0	
Round 1	Kirby Muxloe	0	Pelsall Villa	2	
Round 1	Leiston	3	Henley Town	2	
Round 1	Leverstock Green	3	North Greenford United	1	
Round 1	London Colney	5	Tiptree United	3	(aet)
Round 1	Long Melford	1	Newmarket Town	2	
Round 1	Marske United	2	St Helens Town	3	
Round 1	Merstham	1	Three Bridges	2	
Round 1	Mile Oak	0	Slade Green	0	(aet)
Round 1	Nantwich Town	1	Boldmere St Michaels	0	
Round 1	Needham Market	1	Dereham Town	0	
Round 1	Newcastle Benfield Bay Plastics	3	Whickham	1	
Round 1	Newcastle Town	3	Glapwell	2	
Round 1	Newport Pagnell Town	0	Romford	1	
Round 1	Newton Abbot	1	Corsham Town	0	
Round 1	North Leigh	0	Maidstone United	4	
Round 1	Oldbury United	0	Coleshill Town	4	
Round 1	Oldham Town	3	Seaham Red Star	1	
Round 1	Oxford City	1	Welwyn Garden City	3	
Round 1	Parkgate	3	Liversedge	3	(aet)
Round 1	Poole Town	1	Bideford	2	
Round 1	Racing Club Warwick	1	Barwell	0	
Round 1	Retford United	4	Brodsworth MW	0	
Round 1	Rocester	0	Carlton Town	2	
Round 1	Selby Town	3	South Normanton Athletic	1	
Round 1	Shortwood United	0	Bishop's Cleeve	3	
Round 1	Sidley United	3	Shoreham	0	
Round 1	Squires Gate	3	Salford City	0	
Round 1	Stanway Rovers	4	Basildon United	3	
Round 1	Street	0	Christchurch	2	
Round 1	Sunderland Nissan	1	Abbey Hey	0	
Round 1	Tavistock	3	Penryn Athletic	0	
Round 1	Thatcham Town	4	Selsey	2	(aet)
Round 1	Tilbury	2	Burnham Ramblers	1	
Round 1	Trafford	1	Prudhoe Town	0	
Round 1	Truro City	3	Witney United	1	
Round 1	VT	1	Hythe Town	2	
Round 1	Wantage Town	1	Thamesmead Town	3	
Round 1	Wellington	0	Alvechurch	1	
Round 1	Wellington Town	1	Bemerton Heath Harlequins	2	
Round 1	Welton Rovers	2	Willand Rovers	3	(aet)
Round 1	West Auckland Town	0	Billingham Synthonia	2	
Round 1	Westfields	1	Bridgnorth Town	0	
Round 1	Whitstable Town	1	Andover	3	
Round 1	Wimborne Town	3	Radstock Town	1	
Round 1	Witham Town	5	Waltham Abbey	3	
Round 1	Woodford United	3	Broxbourne Borough V&E	4	
Round 1	Wootton Blue Cross	2	Royston Town	1	

Round 1	Yaxley	8	Southend Manor	1	
Replay	Chalfont St Peter	2	Felixstowe & Walton United	1	
Replay	Dawlish Town	3	Chard Town	2	(aet)
Replay	Dunston Federation Brewery	3	Darlington Railway Athletic	0	
Replay	Liversedge	3	Parkgate	0	
Replay	Pewsey Vale	1	Devizes Town	1	(aet)
	Devizes Town won on penalties				
Replay	Slade Green	1	Mile Oak	4	
Replay	Thornaby	4	Ashington	3	
Round 2	AFC Hornchurch	1	Soham Town Rangers	3	
Round 2	AFC Sudbury	4	Romford	0	
Round 2	Arnold Town	2	Pelsall Villa	0	
Round 2	Barrow Town	1	Quorn	3	
Round 2	Bemerton Heath Harlequins	2	St Blazey	3	
Round 2	Bicester Town	0	Dorking	1	
Round 2	Biddulph Victoria	1	Leamington	2	
Round 2	Bishop's Cleeve	3	Newton Abbot	0	
Round 2	Bodmin Town	3	Bitton	0	
Round 2	Bournemouth	1	Frome Town	0	(aet)
Round 2	Bridgwater Town	0	Slimbridge	1	
Round 2	Brockenhurst	2	Egham Town	2	(aet)
Round 2	Bury Town	3	Hanwell Town	0	
Round 2	Buxton	4	Alvechurch	0	
Round 2	Chasetown	0	Nantwich Town	1	
Round 2	Chessington & Hook United	2	Carterton	0	
Round 2	Christchurch	3	Truro City	2	
Round 2	Colliers Wood United	2	VCD Athletic	3	
Round 2	Colne	4	Norton & Stockton Ancients	0	
Round 2	Concord Rangers	1	Welwyn Garden City	2	(aet)
Round 2	Crook Town	4	Billingham Town	0	
Round 2	Dawlish Town	1	Bideford	2	(aet)
Round 2	Desborough Town	0	Coalville Town	1	
Round 2	Devizes Town	2	Brislington	1	
Round 2	Didcot Town	7	Herne Bay	0	
Round 2	Ford Sports Daventry	4	Coleshill Town	2	
Round 2	Friar Lane & Epworth	1	Stourbridge	5	
Round 2	Glasshoughton Welfare	1	Squires Gate	2	
Round 2	Glossop North End	3	Carlton Town	4	
Round 2	Gorleston	0	Mildenhall Town	0	(aet)
Round 2	Harrogate Railway	0	Cammell Laird	1	
Round 2	Highfield Rangers	2	Gedling Town	3	
Round 2	Highworth Town	0	Wimborne Town	1	
Round 2	Hythe Town	3	Thatcham Town	2	
Round 2	Kingsbury Town	1	Hassocks	0	
Round 2	Ledbury Town	0	Willand Rovers	4	
Round 2	Leverstock Green	0	Chalfont St Peter	2	
Round 2	Liversedge	5	Billingham Synthonia	4	(aet)
Round 2	London Colney	6	Ipswich Wanderers	3	
Round 2	Lowestoft Town	2	Wootton Blue Cross	0	
Round 2	Maidstone United	4	Andover	0	
Round 2	Mile Oak	1	Deal Town	3	(aet)
Round 2	Needham Market	3	Potton United	1	
Round 2	Nelson	0	Ashville	1	
Round 2	Newcastle Benfield Bay Plastics	5	Thornaby	1	
Round 2	Newcastle Town	1	Cradley Town	0	
Round 2	Newmarket Town	2	Tilbury	1	(aet)

Round 2	Pickering Town	1	Oldham Town	0	(aet)
Round 2	Retford United	2	Trafford	1	
Round 2	Rye & Iden United	2	Hillingdon Borough	2	(aet)
Round 2	Selby Town	3	Westfields	3	(aet)
Round 2	Sidley United	4	Erith Town	2	
Round 2	Skelmersdale United	4	West Allotment Celtic	3	
Round 2	St Helens Town	1	Dunston Federation Brewery	3	
Round 2	Stanway Rovers	5	Broxbourne Borough V&E	5	(aet)
Round 2	Sunderland Nissan	3	Bedlington Terriers	3	(aet)
Round 2	Tavistock	4	Backwell United	2	(aet)
Round 2	Thackley	3	Jarrow Roofing Boldon CA	0	
Round 2	Thamesmead Town	0	Brook House	4	
Round 2	Three Bridges	0	Arundel	1	
Round 2	Tipton Town	0	Racing Club Warwick	2	
Round 2	Winchester City	5	AFC Newbury	0	
Round 2	Wisbech Town	8	Leiston	1	
Round 2	Yaxley	3	Witham Town	0	
Replay	Bedlington Terriers	2	Sunderland Nissan	1	
Replay	Broxbourne Borough V&E	3	Stanway Rovers	0	
Replay	Egham Town	0	Brockenhurst	1	
Replay	Hillingdon Borough	1	Rye & Iden United	0	
Replay	Mildenhall Town	2	Gorleston	0	
Replay	Westfields	2	Selby Town	3	(aet)
Round 3	AFC Sudbury	3	Bodmin Town	1	
Round 3	Arundel	1	VCD Athletic	2	
Round 3	Ashville	3	Racing Club Warwick	3	(aet)
Round 3	Bournemouth	1	Brockenhurst	2	
Round 3	Cammell Laird	3	Retford United	0	
Round 3	Coalville Town	3	Arnold Town	3	(aet)
Round 3	Crook Town	8	Ford Sports Daventry	2	
Round 3	Deal Town	2	Tavistock	4	
Round 3	Didcot Town	4	Mildenhall Town	4	(aet)
Round 3	Dorking	5	Christchurch	2	
Round 3	Gedling Town	4	Carlton Town	3	
Round 3	Hillingdon Borough	2	Bideford	1	
Round 3	Hythe Town	2	Chalfont St Peter	1	
Round 3	Leamington	2	Liversedge	1	
Round 3	London Colney	1	Chessington & Hook United	2	
Round 3	Lowestoft Town	2	Kingsbury Town	0	
Round 3	Maidstone United	2	Broxbourne Borough V&E	2	(aet)
Round 3	Needham Market	3	Devizes Town	0	
Round 3	Newcastle Benfield Bay Plastics	2	Stourbridge	1	
Round 3	Newcastle Town	1	Bedlington Terriers	3	
Round 3	Newmarket Town	1	Willand Rovers	0	
Round 3	Pickering Town	1	Dunston Federation Brewery	0	
Round 3	Quorn	0	Nantwich Town	1	
Round 3	Selby Town	0	Buxton	1	
Round 3	Sidley United	1	St Blazey	2	
Round 3	Soham Town Rangers	1	Bury Town	2	
Round 3	Squires Gate	2	Skelmersdale United	1	
Round 3	Thackley	2	Colne	1	
Round 3	Welwyn Garden City	3	Slimbridge	1	
Round 3	Wimborne Town	4	Bishop's Cleeve	1	
Round 3	Wisbech Town	4	Brook House	4	(aet)
Round 3	Yaxley	2	Winchester City	4	

Replay	Arnold Town	3	Coalville Town	0	
Replay	Brook House	2	Wisbech Town	0	
Replay	Broxbourne Borough V&E	3	Maidstone United	3	(aet)
	Broxbourne Borough V&E won on penalties				
Replay	Mildenhall Town	2	Didcot Town	1	
Replay	Racing Club Warwick	2	Ashville	2	(aet)
	Ashville won on penalties				
Round 4	AFC Sudbury	1	Bedlington Terriers	1	(aet)
Round 4	Bedlington Terriers	1	AFC Sudbury	3	
Round 4	Brockenhurst	0	Bury Town	2	
Round 4	Buxton	1	Ashville	0	
Round 4	Chessington & Hook United	1	Cammell Laird	2	
Round 4	Crook Town	3	St Blazey	0	
Round 4	Dorking	1	Mildenhall Town	3	
Round 4	Hillingdon Borough	2	Brook House	0	
Round 4	Hythe Town	1	Winchester City	3	
Round 4	Leamington	2	Wimborne Town	3	
Round 4	Needham Market	3	Nantwich Town	6	(aet)
Round 4	Newcastle Benfield Bay Plastics	3	Lowestoft Town	1	
Round 4	Newmarket Town	2	Welwyn Garden City	2	(aet)
Round 4	Pickering Town	3	Tavistock	0	
Round 4	Squires Gate	2	Gedling Town	1	(aet)
Round 4	Thackley	0	Arnold Town	2	
Round 4	VCD Athletic	1	Broxbourne Borough V&E	0	
Replay	Welwyn Garden City	2	Newmarket Town	1	
	Welwyn Garden City were disqualified for fielding an ineligible player				
Round 5	AFC Sudbury	0	Bury Town	2	
Round 5	Arnold Town	0	Crook Town	1	
Round 5	Cammell Laird	1	VCD Athletic	0	
Round 5	Hillingdon Borough	4	Mildenhall Town	0	
Round 5	Nantwich Town	1	Buxton	0	
Round 5	Squires Gate	2	Newcastle Benfield Bay Plastics	1	
Round 5	Wimborne Town	1	Pickering Town	2	
Round 5	Winchester City	3	Newmarket Town	4	(aet)
Round 6	Crook Town	0	Bury Town	1	
Round 6	Hillingdon Borough	2	Squires Gate	0	
Round 6	Nantwich Town	2	Pickering Town	0	
Round 6	Newmarket Town	1	Cammell Laird	2	

SEMI-FINALS

1st leg	Bury Town	1	Hillingdon Borough	1	
2nd leg	Hillingdon Borough	2	Bury Town	1	
1st leg	Cammell Laird	0	Nantwich Town	1	
2nd leg	Nantwich Town	4	Cammell Laird	0	
FINAL	Nantwich Town	3	Hillingdon Borough	1	

Nationwide Conference South Fixtures 2006/2007	Basingstoke Town	Bedford Town	Bishop's Stortford	Bognor Regis Town	Braintree Town	Cambridge City	Dorchester Town	Eastbourne Borough	Eastleigh	Farnborough Town	Fisher Athletic	Havant & Waterlooville	Hayes	Histon	Lewes	Newport County	Salisbury City	Sutton United	Thurrock	Welling United	Weston-super-Mare	Yeading
Basingstoke Town	■	02/09	09/04	27/01	28/10	26/08	02/12	21/04	26/12	30/12	10/03	11/11	10/02	24/02	06/01	31/03	07/10	17/03	12/08	23/09	22/08	12/09
Bedford Town	16/12	■	22/08	11/11	20/01	01/01	07/10	13/01	12/08	10/02	24/02	09/09	06/03	31/03	02/12	26/08	16/09	04/11	03/03	21/04	09/04	17/03
Bishop's Stortford	28/08	14/04	■	24/03	06/03	20/01	07/04	19/08	09/12	28/10	15/08	16/09	09/09	21/10	28/04	16/12	13/01	17/02	01/01	18/11	03/02	10/03
Bognor Regis Town	16/09	03/02	12/08	■	13/01	09/09	21/04	09/12	17/02	17/03	16/12	01/01	20/01	26/08	09/04	04/11	18/11	06/03	22/08	03/03	06/10	31/03
Braintree Town	03/03	12/09	30/12	23/09	■	31/03	24/02	07/10	02/09	26/08	11/11	02/12	04/11	26/12	17/03	10/02	21/04	12/08	09/04	06/01	27/01	22/08
Cambridge City	07/04	26/12	12/09	06/01	15/08	■	23/09	28/08	18/11	27/01	14/04	24/03	19/08	30/12	02/09	07/10	03/02	03/03	17/02	09/12	04/11	21/04
Dorchester Town	17/02	28/04	26/08	21/10	09/12	13/01	■	16/12	22/08	12/08	09/09	20/01	16/09	17/03	03/03	01/01	06/03	18/11	04/11	03/02	31/03	09/04
Eastbourne Borough	21/10	23/09	17/03	24/02	28/04	09/04	02/09	■	30/12	06/01	02/12	10/02	11/11	27/01	26/12	03/03	04/11	22/08	31/03	12/09	26/08	12/08
Eastleigh	01/01	23/03	24/02	02/12	16/12	10/02	14/04	06/03	■	10/03	07/04	28/08	15/08	28/10	11/11	13/01	20/01	09/09	16/09	19/08	21/04	06/10
Farnborough Town	06/03	18/11	03/03	19/08	07/04	16/09	24/03	09/09	04/11	■	13/01	14/04	16/12	28/04	21/10	20/01	15/08	01/01	09/12	28/08	17/02	03/02
Fisher Athletic	04/11	09/12	31/03	02/09	03/02	21/08	06/01	17/02	26/08	23/09	■	28/04	21/10	11/09	30/12	12/08	03/03	09/04	18/11	26/12	17/03	27/01
Havant & Waterloo.	03/02	06/01	27/01	26/12	17/02	12/08	11/09	18/11	09/04	21/08	06/10	■	03/03	23/09	26/08	17/03	09/12	31/03	21/04	04/11	01/09	30/12
Hayes	18/11	30/12	06/01	12/09	10/03	17/03	27/01	03/02	31/03	02/09	21/04	28/10	■	12/08	22/08	09/04	17/02	09/12	26/08	07/10	23/09	26/12
Histon	09/12	16/08	21/04	07/04	01/01	07/03	19/08	16/09	03/03	07/10	20/01	13/01	24/03	■	04/11	09/09	28/08	03/02	16/12	14/04	18/11	17/02
Lewes	09/09	17/02	06/10	28/08	19/08	16/12	28/10	01/01	03/02	21/04	07/03	07/04	14/04	10/03	■	16/09	23/03	13/01	20/01	16/08	09/12	18/11
Newport County	16/08	07/04	01/09	10/03	18/11	28/04	26/12	28/10	23/09	13/09	23/03	19/08	28/08	06/01	27/01	■	14/04	21/10	03/02	17/02	30/12	09/12
Salisbury City	28/04	27/01	23/09	10/02	21/10	11/11	30/12	10/03	12/09	31/03	28/10	24/02	02/12	09/04	12/08	22/08	■	26/08	17/03	01/09	26/12	06/01
Sutton United	19/08	10/03	02/12	30/12	24/03	28/10	10/02	14/04	06/01	26/12	28/08	15/08	24/02	11/11	23/09	21/04	07/04	■	07/10	27/01	12/09	02/09
Thurrock	23/03	28/10	26/12	14/04	28/08	02/12	10/03	14/08	27/01	24/02	10/02	21/10	07/04	01/09	11/09	11/11	19/08	28/04	■	30/12	06/01	23/09
Welling United	13/01	21/10	10/02	28/10	09/09	24/02	11/11	20/01	17/03	09/04	01/01	10/03	28/04	22/08	31/03	02/12	16/12	16/09	06/03	■	12/08	26/08
Weston-super-Mare	14/04	28/08	11/11	28/04	16/09	10/03	16/08	07/04	21/10	02/12	19/08	16/12	13/01	10/02	24/02	07/03	01/01	20/01	09/09	24/03	■	28/10
Yeading	20/01	19/08	04/11	15/08	14/04	21/10	28/08	24/03	28/04	11/11	16/09	06/03	01/01	02/12	10/02	24/02	09/09	16/12	13/01	07/04	03/03	■

Nationwide Conference North Fixtures 2006/2007	Alfreton Town	Barrow	Blyth Spartans	Droylsden	Farsley Celtic	Gainsborough Trinity	Harrogate Town	Hinckley United	Hucknall Town	Hyde United	Kettering Town	Lancaster City	Leigh RMI	Moor Green	Nuneaton Borough	Redditch United	Scarborough	Stalybridge Celtic	Vauxhall Motors	Worcester City	Workington	Worksop Town
Alfreton Town	■	18/11	17/03	06/01	10/03	28/10	01/09	31/03	26/12	22/08	06/10	12/08	27/01	16/09	09/12	21/04	06/03	03/02	17/02	09/04	26/08	30/12
Barrow	10/02	■	31/03	26/08	24/02	13/01	22/08	11/11	17/03	09/04	16/12	01/01	04/11	07/10	21/04	09/09	03/03	23/09	20/01	12/08	12/09	02/12
Blyth Spartans	19/08	15/08	■	16/09	28/08	18/11	30/12	28/04	06/01	06/03	09/12	21/10	02/09	28/10	03/02	24/03	26/12	07/04	14/04	27/01	17/02	10/03
Droylsden	09/09	07/04	13/01	■	24/03	09/12	21/04	16/12	18/11	07/10	23/09	17/02	03/02	14/04	19/08	14/08	04/11	11/09	01/01	03/03	20/01	28/08
Farsley Celtic	04/11	09/12	09/04	12/08	■	17/02	26/12	17/03	16/09	26/08	18/11	22/08	31/03	02/09	27/01	07/10	30/12	03/03	03/02	06/01	21/04	06/03
Gainsborough Trinity	03/03	16/09	10/02	24/02	02/12	■	06/03	12/08	30/12	06/01	04/11	17/03	09/04	27/01	03/09	11/11	31/03	28/04	21/10	26/08	22/08	26/12
Harrogate Town	16/12	14/04	12/09	21/10	01/01	20/01	■	09/09	10/03	28/10	28/08	13/01	18/11	24/03	17/02	07/04	03/02	19/08	23/09	28/04	09/12	15/08
Hinckley United	14/08	03/02	07/10	02/09	19/08	24/03	06/01	■	09/12	21/04	14/04	03/03	16/09	30/12	26/12	28/08	17/02	28/11	07/04	05/03	04/11	27/01
Hucknall Town	01/01	19/08	09/09	10/02	13/01	12/09	04/11	24/02	■	11/11	15/08	20/01	03/03	02/12	28/08	14/04	28/04	24/03	16/12	21/10	23/09	07/04
Hyde United	14/04	28/08	20/01	28/04	07/04	09/09	03/03	21/10	03/02	■	25/03	16/12	17/02	14/08	18/11	23/09	09/12	01/01	11/09	04/11	13/01	19/08
Kettering Town	28/04	02/09	24/02	27/01	10/02	10/03	09/04	22/08	31/03	12/08	■	26/08	06/01	06/03	30/12	02/12	16/09	21/10	28/10	26/12	17/03	11/11
Lancaster City	24/03	26/12	21/04	02/12	14/04	19/08	16/09	28/10	06/03	02/09	07/04	■	30/12	10/02	06/01	10/03	27/01	15/08	28/08	11/11	07/10	24/02
Leigh RMI	23/09	10/03	16/12	11/11	15/08	28/08	10/02	13/01	28/10	02/12	09/09	12/09	■	07/04	14/04	19/08	21/10	20/01	23/03	24/02	01/01	28/04
Moor Green	13/01	28/04	03/03	22/08	16/12	23/09	12/08	12/09	17/02	31/03	20/01	18/11	26/08	■	04/11	01/01	09/04	09/09	09/12	17/03	03/02	21/10
Nuneaton Borough	24/02	21/10	11/11	17/03	23/09	16/12	02/12	01/01	09/04	10/02	12/09	09/09	22/08	10/03	■	20/01	26/08	13/01	28/04	31/03	12/08	28/10
Redditch United	21/10	06/01	12/08	31/03	28/04	03/02	26/08	09/04	22/08	27/01	17/02	04/11	17/03	26/12	06/03	■	02/09	09/12	18/11	30/12	03/03	16/09
Scarborough	20/01	28/10	01/01	10/03	12/09	15/08	11/11	02/12	06/10	24/02	13/01	23/09	21/04	28/08	07/04	16/12	■	14/04	19/08	10/02	09/09	23/03
Stalybridge Celtic	11/11	27/01	26/08	30/12	28/10	07/10	17/03	10/02	12/08	26/12	21/04	31/03	06/03	06/01	16/09	24/02	22/08	■	10/03	02/12	09/04	02/09
Vauxhall Motors	02/12	06/03	22/08	26/12	11/11	21/04	27/01	26/08	01/09	30/12	03/03	09/04	12/08	24/02	06/10	10/02	17/03	04/11	■	16/09	31/03	06/01
Worcester City	28/08	23/03	23/09	28/10	09/09	07/04	06/10	20/01	21/04	10/03	01/01	03/02	09/12	19/08	14/08	11/09	18/11	17/02	13/01	■	16/12	14/04
Workington	07/04	30/12	02/12	06/03	21/10	14/04	24/02	10/03	27/01	16/09	19/08	28/04	26/12	11/11	23/03	28/10	06/01	28/08	15/08	01/09	■	10/02
Worksop Town	12/09	17/02	04/11	09/04	20/01	01/01	31/03	23/09	26/08	17/03	03/02	09/12	06/10	21/04	03/03	13/01	12/08	16/12	09/09	22/08	18/11	■

Nationwide Conference South Fixtures 2006/2007

	Basingstoke Town	Bedford Town	Bishop's Stortford	Bognor Regis Town	Braintree Town	Cambridge City	Dorchester Town	Eastbourne Borough	Eastleigh	Farnborough Town	Fisher Athletic	Havant & Waterlooville	Hayes	Histon	Lewes	Newport County	Salisbury City	Sutton United	Thurrock	Welling United	Weston-super-Mare	Yeading
Basingstoke Town		02/09	09/04	27/01	28/10	26/08	02/12	21/04	26/12	30/12	10/03	11/11	10/02	24/02	06/01	31/03	07/10	17/03	12/08	23/09	22/08	12/09
Bedford Town	16/12		22/08	11/11	20/01	01/01	07/10	13/01	12/08	10/02	24/02	09/09	06/03	31/03	02/12	26/08	16/09	04/11	03/03	21/04	09/04	17/03
Bishop's Stortford	28/08	14/04		24/03	06/03	20/01	07/04	19/08	09/12	28/10	15/08	16/09	09/09	21/10	28/04	16/12	13/01	17/02	01/01	18/11	03/02	10/03
Bognor Regis Town	16/09	03/02	12/08		13/01	09/09	21/04	09/12	17/02	17/03	16/12	01/01	20/01	26/08	09/04	04/11	18/11	06/03	22/08	03/03	06/10	31/03
Braintree Town	03/03	12/09	30/12	23/09		31/03	24/02	07/10	02/09	26/08	11/11	02/12	04/11	26/12	17/03	10/02	21/04	12/08	09/04	06/01	27/01	22/08
Cambridge City	07/04	26/12	12/09	06/01	15/08		23/09	28/08	18/11	27/01	14/04	24/03	19/08	30/12	02/09	07/10	03/02	03/03	17/02	09/12	04/11	21/04
Dorchester Town	17/02	28/04	26/08	21/10	09/12	13/01		16/12	22/08	12/08	09/09	20/01	16/09	17/03	03/03	01/01	06/03	18/11	04/11	03/02	31/03	09/04
Eastbourne Borough	21/10	23/09	17/03	24/02	28/04	09/04	02/09		30/12	06/01	02/12	10/02	11/11	27/01	26/12	03/03	04/11	22/08	31/03	12/09	26/08	12/08
Eastleigh	01/01	23/03	24/02	02/12	16/12	10/02	14/04	06/03		10/03	07/04	28/08	15/08	28/10	11/11	13/01	20/01	09/09	16/09	19/08	21/04	06/10
Farnborough Town	06/03	18/11	03/03	19/08	07/04	16/09	24/03	09/09	04/11		13/01	14/04	16/12	28/04	21/10	20/01	15/08	01/01	09/12	28/08	17/02	03/02
Fisher Athletic	04/11	09/12	31/03	02/09	03/02	21/08	06/01	17/02	26/08	23/09		28/04	21/10	11/09	30/12	12/08	03/03	09/04	18/11	26/12	17/03	27/01
Havant & Waterloo.	03/02	06/01	27/01	26/12	17/02	12/08	11/09	18/11	09/04	21/08	06/10		03/03	23/09	26/08	17/03	09/12	31/03	21/04	04/11	01/09	30/12
Hayes	18/11	30/12	06/01	12/09	10/03	17/03	27/01	03/02	31/03	02/09	21/04	28/10		12/08	22/08	09/04	17/02	09/12	26/08	07/10	23/09	26/12
Histon	09/12	16/08	21/04	07/04	01/01	07/03	19/08	16/09	03/03	07/10	20/01	13/01	24/03		04/11	09/09	28/08	03/02	16/12	14/04	18/11	17/02
Lewes	09/09	17/02	06/10	28/08	19/08	16/12	28/10	01/01	03/02	21/04	07/03	07/04	14/04	10/03		16/09	23/03	13/01	20/01	16/08	09/12	18/11
Newport County	16/08	07/04	01/09	10/03	18/11	28/04	26/12	28/10	23/09	13/09	23/03	19/08	28/08	06/01	27/01		14/04	21/10	03/02	17/02	30/12	09/12
Salisbury City	28/04	27/01	23/09	10/02	21/10	11/11	30/12	10/03	12/09	31/03	28/10	24/02	02/12	09/04	12/08	22/08		26/08	17/03	01/09	26/12	06/01
Sutton United	19/08	10/03	02/12	30/12	24/03	28/10	10/02	14/04	06/01	26/12	28/08	15/08	24/02	11/11	23/09	21/04	07/04		07/10	27/01	12/09	02/09
Thurrock	23/03	28/10	26/12	14/04	28/08	02/12	10/03	14/08	27/01	24/02	10/02	21/10	07/04	01/09	11/09	11/11	19/08	28/04		30/12	06/01	23/09
Welling United	13/01	21/10	10/02	28/10	09/09	24/02	11/11	20/01	17/03	09/04	01/01	10/03	28/04	22/08	31/03	02/12	16/12	16/09	06/03		12/08	26/08
Weston-super-Mare	14/04	28/08	11/11	28/04	16/09	10/03	16/08	07/04	21/10	02/12	19/08	16/12	13/01	10/02	24/02	07/03	01/01	20/01	09/09	24/03		28/10
Yeading	20/01	19/08	04/11	15/08	14/04	21/10	28/08	24/03	28/04	11/11	16/09	06/03	01/01	02/12	10/02	24/02	09/09	16/12	13/01	07/04	03/03	